GW00399942

REACHING OUT

ARYEH KAPLAN

ISBN 1-879016-01-X

Copyright © 1974 by Aryeh Kaplan
Second edition 1977.
Third edition 1991.

Published by the National Conference of Synagogue Youth/Union of Orthodox Jewish Congregations of America, 45 West 36th Street, New York, NY 10018.

Produced by Olivestone Print Communications, Inc.

PRINTED IN THE UNITED STATES OF AMERICA

Contents

A Publication

in the

JOSEPH TANENBAUM LIBRARY Series

Foreword

Among the efforts NCSY has made to communicate with the leadership and youth of the American Jewish community through the written word, none is more significant than this historic publication. It is a hallmark of the relentless struggle we have waged for over fifteen years to demonstrate that a thesis of despair is unfounded and indefensible.

We have witnessed literally thousands of young people who have been inspired to return to Jewish tradition and enter schools of Torah study. With an organizational structure encompassing eighteen regions from coast to coast, NCSY reaches out to tens of thousands of Jewish youth. But even more significant than all this is the evidence that a movement for return to authentic Jewish sources on a mass scale is both feasible and necessary.

We have effectively demonstrated that Jewish youth can be inspired to identify, practice and live a life of vibrant Jewish commitment. NCSY has succeeded uniquely in reinforcing the loyalties of youth from Orthodox backgrounds, as well as in redirecting thousands of young people from utterly non-religious homes to a life of Jewish thought and observance.

The young Baal Teshuva is no longer an isolated oddity. Regained for their people and faith, hundreds have gone on from NCSY experience to yeshivos and other institutions of higher Jewish learning. Many have become rabbis, teachers, youth leaders—and even Roshei Yeshiva—with tremendous impact on both the youth and adult communities. The significance of this phenomenon can only be measured in historic terms.

What NCSY has done has been to tap the unique human resources of the day school and yeshiva movement to infuse spiritual and intellectual direction into a vast nationwide program of Jewish rediscovery. This has resulted in an effective Jewish renaissance among tens of thousands of alienated and often antagonistic youth.

The new climate that has been created by these and similar efforts must challenge our leadership to re-examine our priorities. New vistas must be created to meet the yearning of Jewish youth for the Torah way of life.

The challenges that confront us may be fraught with danger. But they hold great promise, and must be met with vision, energy and effective action. Thousands of our deeply committed people must be inspired to respond to the call to reach out, and quench the widespread thirst for Jewish living among our young people.

The Prophet Amos says (8:11/12):

> *Behold, days are coming, says the Lord God*
> *I will send famine to the land;*
> *Not hunger for bread, or thirst for water*
> *But for hearing God's words*
> *They shall stagger from north to south*
> *From east to west*
> *Seeking God's words*
> *But they shall not find it*

But if they do not find it, whose responsibility will it be? Can we then remain silent?

RABBI PINCHAS STOLPER
1974/5734

Introduction

One of today's important developments is the fact that there are thousands of young Jews seeking their roots. Traveling across the country, we come across hundreds of Jewish youth, who, after generations of alienation, have finally returned to the Judaism of their forefathers. But this development should not make us complacent. For every one who returns, there are still hundreds who are irreplacebly lost.

Recently, a large segment of the Jewish community has become very alarmed by various missionary groups, such as "Jews for Jesus." Although the missionary problem was a grave one, for the while at least, it was merely the tip of a big iceberg. For every young boy or girl who converted to Christianity, there were over a thousand who were lost to Judaism in any number of other ways.

We live in a time when an alarming and growing majority of our youth is being lost through intermarriage, assimilation, and general alienation. When reports tell us that 80% of our youth never go to synagogue, even on RoshHaShanah and Yom Kippur, something is dramatically wrong. When we find that almost half of our youth are intermarrying, then we know that we are faced with a problem of awesome dimensions.

But what are we doing about it?

One of the serious problems has been the isolation of the Torah community as well as its inability to cope with the problems of American Jewry at large. In too many circles, there is a general feeling that, "as long as I am religious—as long as my own children go to yeshiva—as long as the religious community remains viable—then everything is all right." There are some concerned groups, but they represent only a very small portion of Torah Jewry's resources.

The truth is that as long as Judaism as a whole is declining in America, everything is not all right. No community can divorce itself completely from the world, and the deterioration of Jewish life in general is bound to have effects even in the strongest religious circles. If we do not work to rehabilitate the Jewish community today, then it will be our children and grandchildren who will suffer from our negligence.

Besides this, from a Torah view every Jew has a distinct obligation to look out for the spiritual benefit of his brethren. There is a commandment in the Torah, "You must correct your neighbor." This commandment gives us a definite obligation to speak up when we see other Jews going astray. There is the concept that "All Israel are responsible, one for the other." There is the teaching that, "Anyone who has the opportunity to protest (wrongdoing), and does not do so, is caught up in the sin."

The Gemorah tells us that when the Holy Temple (*Bais HaMikdash*) was destroyed, even the "perfectly righteous" were killed. The reason for this was because they made no effort to lead the "absolutely wicked" to the true path. The Rambam (*Maimonides*) comments that God had promised that they would survive, and that this was the only time that He ever annulled a good decree. The point is thus brought across most strongly that our responsibilities extend beyond our own doorsteps.

One of the things that we hope to do in this book is to point out our obligations as set forth by the greatest Torah authorities. Each section will speak of a different aspect of this problem, and will be followed by a number of readings presenting a translation of these ideas in the original.

In recent generations, as the observance of Yiddishkeit began to weaken, a number of our greatest leaders spoke out against the indifference of the religious community toward those who had strayed. Most prominent of these was the saintly Chafetz Chaim (Rabbi Yisroel Meir HaCohen), who wrote numerous essays on the subject. Joining him were such luminaries as Rabbi Yosef Hurwitz, Rosh Yeshiva of Navaradok, and Rabbi Samson Raphael Hirsch. From the writings of these giants, we see that the teachings regarding mutual responsibility were not meant to be mere theory, but to have numerous practical applications as well. A translation of a number of these sources is included toward the end of this work.

Besides the moral issue, there are important issues involving Jewish Law, especially since the Torah commandment, "You must correct your neighbor," comes into play. In the final section, we will present a summary of these laws, as expounded by our sages throughout the generations.

It might seem presumptuous for me, relatively unknown in the circles of Torah leadership, to speak out on this issue. But in recent months, such *Gedolim* as "Reb Moshe" Feinstein have spoken out, declaring that even Yeshiva students have an obliga- tion to devote some time to help bring others back to Yiddishkeit. I had the privilege of transcribing and translating Rabbi Fein- stein's talk for publication in the *Jewish Observer,* and have in- cluded it in this collection.

In the case of Yeshiva students, a special "dispensation" *(Heter)* may be needed to permit them to take time for their sacred studies to work with our nonreligious brethren. But those who are not immersed in Torah study certainly have always had the obligation to be concerned with the uncommitted. Every one of us must find his or her way to respond to the unspoken cry for help that is in the hearts, if not on the lips, of our estranged brethren.

ARYEH KAPLAN
Rosh Chodesh Iyar, 5734

I
Love Means Reaching Out

What is the most important verse in the Torah? Of course one may argue that all verses are equally holy and important but then, as some old Southerners used to say, "Some are more equal than others." Even though every verse in the Torah is the word of God, there is no question that some are stressed more than others.

There is one verse in the Torah that is emphasized more than all the others. The Torah itself commands us to recite it twice every day, to bind it in the Tefillin on our arms, and to write it on the Mezuzah on our doorposts. Throughout our history, it was the first verse a Jew was taught as a child, and the last he uttered before he died. It is the cry that was on the lips of our countless martyrs as they gave their lives for God.

By now, the identity of this verse should be obvious. It is the *Sh'ma (Deuteronomy 6:4)*, "Hear O Israel, HaShem is our God, HaShem is One."

Most of us are aware that this is the most basic declaration of our faith. We exclaim that we believe in God, that He is concerned with us—He is "our God"—and that He alone is the One True God.

But before we make this most important of all declarations, we include another short phrase: "Hear O Israel." It is not enough for a person to declare "HaShem is our God, HaShem is One." We must call out and proclaim this truth to all Israel—"Hear O Israel."

If a person truly believes in God, then he cannot remain indifferent when others do not share this belief. When a person is in possession of a great truth, then he wants to share it with others. When one has access to the greatest Truth in the world, such sharing becomes imperative.

Right after this verse, the Torah goes on to tell us, "You shall love HaShem your God, with all your heart, with all your soul, and with all your might." This statement that we must love God is one of the 613 commandments of the Torah.

But when we ponder this as a commandment, it becomes somewhat difficult to understand. Love is an emotion. It is something that we feel. How can the Torah command us to feel the emotion of love? What does such a commandment mean?

Another difficult question involves the expression of this love. When we love a person, there are many ways in which we can show our love. But how do we express our love for God?

Our sages teach us that one of the prime ways of observing this commandment and expressing this love is by bringing other people to God.

When we teach others about God and bring them to observe His commandments, then we are expressing our own love for Him.

When you like a person very much, then you also want others to like him. You want others to know his worth and see his good points. When you truly love a person, you want the whole world to know how wonderful that person is. Should it be any different when you love God?

There are many people who are observant and keep the Torah's commandments. But people can do so for a great variety of reasons. Some do it because they were brought up that way, and keep it out of sheer habit. Others do it because they are part of a religious society, and for them, being religious is merely a form of conformity. As the *Mesilas Yesharim* points out, individuals such as these could not be expected to care whether or not others keep the Torah or are aware of God's commandments.[1] If a person is religious because of habit or conformity, then he will not be at all concerned about those who are not part of his society.

But there are also people who are religious on a much deeper and more profound level. For them Judaism is something very real, and their feelings toward God run very deep. Every time they observe one of God's commandments, it is an expression of their love of God. Such a person cannot look away when others are indifferent to God and His teachings. If they could they would shout it from the rooftops. This is what our sages mean when they teach us that the true expression of our love for God is to bring others to Him.

In a sense, we see this from the verses themselves. In the first verse the Torah says, "Hear O Israel, HaShem is our God, HaShem is One." Here, we see that we cannot merely keep our belief to ourselves, but must proclaim it out loud—"Hear O Israel." The next verse tells us that this is also an expression of loving God, "with all your heart, with all your soul, and with all your might."

Our sages teach us that there are two ways in which we can bring others to love God. The simplest is by example. If a person truly loves God, then he will not disgrace Him by his actions. He will not do anything that will make people despise God's teachings. Rather, he will behave in an exemplary manner, so that his example alone will attract others to observe God's commandments. This is a constant obligation for every Jew.

But besides this, the commandment to love God also gives us an obligation to actually reach out and bring others to God. We must talk to people and teach them, doing everything in our power to make God and His Torah known to all our brethren. This also, as our sages teach us, is included in the commandment to love God.

The *Sifri* (see readings at the end of this chapter) says that in this respect, we must emulate Abraham's love of God, for it was in this respect that Abraham differed from all the other righteous people of his time. The others may have served God, but they were content to do so by themselves, secluded away from all mankind, and they did not express any concern if others were not aware of God and His teachings. Only Abraham reached out, and drew people "under the wings of the Divine Presence." It was because of this that of all the great individuals of antiquity, only Abraham was worthy of becoming the father of the Jewish people.

This is a most important point. The Jewish people only came into existence as they did because Abraham reached out and tried to teach the entire civilized world about God. If we are to be worthy of being called His children then we can do no less.

On a deeper level, when a person tries to bring others to love God, this also intensifies his own love. The more a person tries to bring others to keep the Torah, the more he himself is imbued with a feeling for its depth and significance. Even if he is unsuc-cessful in influencing others, he himself may be influenced most deeply.

Since bringing others to love God also intensifies a person's own love, when he does this, he is literally observing the command-ment, "You shall love HaShem your God."

Besides telling us to love God, the Torah also commands us (Leviticus 19:18), "You shall love your neighbor as yourself." So important is this commandment that Rabbi Akiva was to declare it, "the main point of the Torah" (Klal Gadol BaTorah).[2]

There are many ways in which we can express our love for our fellow man. This includes every type of kindness and charity, and also tells us that we must be totally concerned with the needs of others, even beyond the requirements of the Law. As Hillel explained it, we must not do anything to another that we would not want done to ourselves.[3]

But if we must be concerned about others on a material and psychological level, how much more so must we express this concern on a spiritual level! If we really feel that keeping the Torah and observing God's commandments are the most impor-tant things in the world, how can we remain indifferent to those who are ignorant of them? If we saw a person destroying his body of ignorance, would it not be an act of love to enlighten him? Should we act any differently when a person is destroying his soul?

According to Rabbi Eliahu, the Vilna Gaon, the most profound expression of our love for others is "bringing them close to the Torah."[4] In his commentary, he says that this is the underlying sense of the Mishnah, "Hillel said: Be like students of Aaron— love peace, pursue peace, love people, and draw them close to the Torah."[5]

In *Avos DeRabbi Nathan,* we find that Hillel was also teaching us to emulate Abraham in this respect: "A person should go around and bring people under the wings of the Divine Presence, just like Abraham did."[6]

We therefore see that when a person brings others to Torah, he is expressing the two most basic kinds of love—that toward God, and that toward his fellow man. If a person has two dear friends, he will try to bring them together. When a person loves both God and man, then he also tries to bring the two together.

In correcting others and bringing them to the Truth, a person also emulates God. It is written *(Proverbs 3:12),* "God corrects those whom He loves, just like a father (corrects) a child whom he cherishes."[7] If we think about it, the love of God toward man is the greatest love possible. Just as God Himself is infinite, so is His love infinite, and indeed, God Himself calls his love *Ahavas Olam*—an "infinite love."[8]

Therefore, if a person truly wishes to express his love of man, the highest way in which he can do so is by emulating God's own love. One of the primary ways in which God expressed this love was His teaching us the Torah, as we say in the evening prayer, "You have loved the house of Israel with an infinite love—You have taught us Torah and *Mitzvos.* . . ." Another manner of ex- pressing this love is by correcting others, even as God Himself does. Both of these involve bringing a person to truth. Since both are emulations of God's own love, they represent the highest possible expression of love for man.

It has been said that the opposite of love is not hate but indifference. If a person truly believes in Torah and Judaism, then he is well aware of what is lacking in the Jew who is oblivious to his heritage. If he truly loves his fellow man, then how can he remain indifferent to such a lack? How can he see a person going astray, and not try to bring him back to the path of Truth?

The first verse of the *Sh'ma* is the most essential statement of a Jew's belief. But if a person truly believes, then he must begin by crying out, "Hear O Israel." For if he really believes then he cannot stand idly by and see other Jews remaining unaware of the great truths of Judaism. If he truly feels that "HaShem is our God, HaShem is One," then he must want the whole world to be aware of this great fact, and must begin by exclaiming, "Hear O Israel."

NOTES

1. *Mesilas Yesharim* 19. See Chafetz Chaim, *Davar BeIto,* chapter 18, quoted in the readings at the end of this book.
2. *Sifri* on Leviticus 19:18, *Yerushalmi Nedarim* 9:4 (30b), *Berashis Rabbah* 24:7.
3. *Shabbos* 31a.
4. *Biurey HaGra* on *Avos* 1:12.
5. *Avos* 1:12.
6. *Avos DeRabbi Nathan* 12:8.
7. See *Zohar* 3:85b, *Reshis Chochmah, Shaar HaAnvah* 5 (228a).
8. Jeremiah 31:3.

READINGS

TALMUD

It is written (*Deuteronomy 6:5*), "You shall love HaShem your God. . ." This means that you should bring the Name of Heaven to be loved by others.

You should study (Torah), review it, and attend the wise, but you must also be perfectly honest in your business dealings and speak pleasantly to all people.

What do people then say? "Happy is this person who studied

Torah. Happy are his parents who taught him Torah. Happy is his teacher who taught him Torah. How unfortunate are those who do not study Torah. See this person. He studied Torah, and look how fine are his ways, how perfect are his deeds."

Regarding such a person, it is written *(Isaiah 49:3)*, "And He said to me: You, Israel, are My servant, with whom I am honored."

But when a person studies (Torah), reviews it, and attends the wise, but does not deal honestly with others, or does not speak pleasantly to all people, then what do people say about him? "Woe is to this person who studied Torah. Woe is to his parents who taught him Torah. Woe is to his teacher who taught him Torah. This person studied Torah and see how unseemly are his deeds, how unethical are his ways."

Regarding such people it is written *(Ezekiel 26:20)*, "(When they come to the nations, they profaned My holy name,) for men said of them: These are God's people, and they have gone forth out of the land."

Yoma 86a

SIFRI

(The *Sifri* was the first Talmudical commentary written on the Books of Numbers and Deuteronomy.)

It is written, "You shall love HaShem your God. . . ." Make all people love Him, just like Abraham your father did.

It is written *(Genesis 12:5)*, "The souls that (Abraham) *made* in Haran." If all the people in the world came together to create even a mosquito and place a soul in it, would they then be able to do so? How then can the Torah speak of "the souls that (Abraham) made in Haran?" But this teaches us that Abraham converted them (to belief in God) and brought them under the wings of the Divine Presence.

Sifri on Deuteronomy 6:5

———◆———

MIDRASH

Rabbi Yosi bar Chanina said: "When people correct each other, it brings them to love each other. It is thus written (*Proverbs 9:8*), "Correct a wise man, and he will love you." In the opinion of Rabbi Yosi bar Chanina, all love that does not include mutual correction is not true love.

Berashis Rabbah 54:3

———◆———

RAMBAM (MAIMONIDES)

Included in the commandment (to love God) is the responsibility that we bring all men to believe in God and serve Him.

When you love another person, you speak of his good points and emphasize them, and you also try to bring others to love him. The same is true when you truly love God. When you have some idea of His true nature, you are certain to try to bring those who are unaware and ignorant to recognize this Truth.

In the words of the *Sifri:* "You shall love HaShem your God— make all people love Him, just like Abraham your father did. . . ."

Abraham truly loved God, as the scripture bears witness (*Isaiah 41:8*), "Abraham who loved Me." Because of Abraham's deep understanding and great love of God, he also brought other people to believe in Him.

In a similar manner, you should love God and bring other people to Him.

Sefer HaMitzvos, Positive No. 3

Abraham was forty years old when he recognized his Creator. As soon as he knew and became aware, he began to reply to the people of Ur, debating with them, and explaining that they were not following the true path. . . He began to teach the people that they should only serve the God of the Universe, and that they should bow only to Him. Thus, all people would come to recognize Him. . . .

Because he won so many people over with his arguments, the king sought to kill him, but he was saved by a miracle, and left for Haran. There he began to call out in a loud voice to all the world, proclaiming that there is One God over the world, and that only He alone should be worshipped.

Abraham taught publicly and gathered people around him. He went from city to city, from nation to nation, until he reached the land of Canaan. There he continued to call out, as it was written (*Genesis 21:33*), (And Abraham planted a tamarisk-tree in Beersheba,) and there he called out in the name of Hashem, God of the universe."

When people gathered around him and asked about what he was teaching, he told each one according to his intellect, bringing them back to the true path. Eventually, he gathered tens of thousands of people, and these became the members of Abraham's household. He planted this foundation in their hearts and wrote books about it.

Yad, Avodas Kochavim 1:3

This is very surprising, because Shem and Eber (who also served God) were there. Why did they not protest (the idolatry of their generation)?

Raavad (Rabbi Avraham ben David) on the above

(In answer to the Raavad's question) Abraham called out and publicly proclaimed the belief in one God. Shem and Eber, on the other hand, only taught the ways of God to their students, but they did not push themselves to go out and proclaim it publicly. It is for this reason that Abraham was greater than they were.

Rabbi Yosef Karo: Kesef Mishneh on the above

◆

RABBI ELAZAR AZKARI: SEFER CHEREDIM

The Commandment, "You shall love HaShem your God," also includes a responsibility that you should talk to others about the Torah and speak convincingly until you bring the love of God into their hearts.

The phrase, "you shall love," therefore has two connotations. It teaches us that we should act in a manner that will also bring others to love God.

The *Sifri* therefore states, "You shall love HaShem your God— make people love Him, just like Abraham your father did. . . ." It is because of this that God called Abraham the one who loved Him, as it is written (*Isaiah 41:8*), "The children of Abraham who love Me."

This is an offshoot (*Anaf*) of the actual Commandment.

Sefer Cheredim 1:9

◆

RABBI MOSHE CHAIM LUZZATTO: MESILAS YESHARIM

The third condition (involved in the love of God) requires action. . . .

Our sages speak most strongly about the person who has the opportunity to protest against wrongdoing and does not do so. They have decreed that the judgement of such a person should be to be caught up in the sin of the wrongdoer himself.

We also find this in the Midrash (*Eicha Rabbah*) on the verse (*Lamentations 1:6*), "(Israel's) princes have become like rams." The Midrash says that in very hot weather, rams hide their faces under the bodies of others. The leaders of Israel likewise saw others sinning, but hid their faces from it. God said, "The time will come when I will do the same to them."

(The need for such action,) however, should be obvious. When you like a person very much, you cannot simply (stand by and) allow others to beat him and insult him. When necessary you do whatever you can to help him. The same is true when you really love God. You cannot stand by and allow others to desecrate His name and violate His commandments.

Mesilas Yesharim 19

———◆———

RABBI LEVI YITZCHOK OF BERDICHOV

There are two types of people who serve God. One serves God with great intensity, but remains by himself and does not attempt to bring the irreligious to serve the Creator. Such a person feels that it is enough if he himself serves God.

There is another type of person, however, who serves God, but also works to bring others to serve Him. Such a person emulates Abraham, who converted people (to belief in God).

We find in the writings of the Ari (Rabbi Yitzchok Luria) that Noah was punished because he did not try to correct the people of his generation. He was therefore reborn as Moses. It was for this reason that Moses constantly worked to correct all Israel.

Our sages speak of one who "is good to heaven and good to people" (*Kiddushin 40a*). This refers to the person who serves God, but who also tries to bring the irreligious to also serve Him. He is "good to heaven" because he serves God. But he is also "good to people" because he brings them to serve the Creator.

Noah, however, did not work to bring others to serve God. . . . The Torah therefore states that (*Genesis 6:9*), "Noah walked with God." This means that Noah walked with God only. He served God by himself, and did not walk with other people, trying to bring them close to God so that they too should be counted among those who serve Him.

Kedushas Levi, beginning of Noah

RABBI NACHMAN OF BRESLOV

When people speak about religion, both Direct Light and Reflected Light are generated.

When you discuss Godliness with a friend, the information that he receives from you is Direct Light. What you gain (from your own words) through him is Reflected Light.

Sometimes you can speak to a person about Godliness, and your words are not accepted. Still, you yourself can be motivated by your own words. Your words literally bounce off from your friend, and are reflected to you.

This is very much like a rubber ball. The reason why a ball bounces from a stone wall is because it cannot penetrate it. Similarly, when the other person refuses to accept what you tell him, your words are reflected to you. You yourself are then influenced by your own words.

These same words may have not had any effect at all on you if you had spoken them to yourself. But when you express them to someone else, and he is not influenced, they are reflected to you. You can then be motivated by your own words.

Likutey Moharan 184

II

A People United

An important concept that we must explore is the basic unity of the Jewish people. Although a Jew serves God as an individual, he cannot do so without being part of the Jewish people as a whole. Our sages teach us that a person who "separates himself from the ways of the community" has no portion in the World to Come—even if he is otherwise a religious Jew.[1] As Rabbi Yonah explains, the reason for this is because he does not partake in the basic unity of the Jewish people.[2]

This is because the Jewish people did not accept the Torah as individuals, but as a community. It is thus written (*Exodus 24:3*), "And all the people answered *with a single voice* and said, 'All the words that God speaks, we will obey.'" Therefore, if a person does not consider himself as one with the Jewish people as a whole, he rejects the oneness with which they accepted the Torah (see readings).

We can also understand this on a somewhat deeper level. Our

sages teach us that we are bound to keep the commandments of the Torah as if each one of us had made an oath to keep them, and indeed, this has important implications in Jewish Law.[3] At first glance, however, this may seem somewhat puzzling. Even if all Jews did make an oath to keep the Torah when they accepted it, how can this oath be binding on us today? There is a general rule that a person can only make an oath for himself, and that he cannot bind future generations with his oath.[4] This being so, why was the oath involved in the acceptance of the Torah any different?

The answer is that an oath made by an entire community is different than an individual oath. The community is considered to be an organic whole, and as long as that community lives, the oath is binding on all of its members.[5] Thus, the very fact that all Israel spoke "with a single voice" is what made the oath binding on all future generations. A person who separates himself from the Jewish people is saying in effect that he is no longer bound by the community's oath to keep the Torah. Even if he keeps it then, he is doing so because of his convenience, and not because of his obligation to God. One must keep the Torah as a Jew and not as an individual.

According to many authorities, the oath itself was proclaimed at Mount Gerizim and Mount Ebal, shortly after the Jews entered the Land of Israel. The Torah tells us that at this time, they were to proclaim (Deuteronomy 27:26), "Cursed is the man who does not uphold the words of this Torah."[6] When all Israel answered Amen to this statement, in effect they made an oath to keep the Torah for all generations.

But the oath was not just that each individual should keep the Torah. It was that the entire Jewish people as a whole should live by it. It is for this reason that the oath speaks of the "man who does not *uphold* the words of this Torah." The Jerusalem Talmud asks, "Can the Torah then fall down," that it needs to be upheld? It answers that this means that the oath was for every individual to make sure that the Torah is upheld by every other Jew.[7] (In a later chapter, we will see how the Chafetz Chaim (Rabbi Yisroel Meir HaCohen) deals with this question.)

From all this, we can begin to see the reason for a statement that will be quoted again and again in this book. Our sages teach us that "All Israel are responsible, one for the other" (Kol Yisrael Arevim Zeh BaZeh). Every Jew has a moral responsibility for the deeds of every other Jew in the world. If even a single Jew does wrong, then every other Jew bears the responsibility for it.

The Gemorah (see readings) derives this from the verse (Leviticus 26:37), "A man shall stumble for his brother." We know however, that whenever the Torah uses the word "stumble" (Kashel), it refers to moral rather than physical stumbling.[8] Therefore, as the Gemorah explains, this verse teaches us that every Jew "stumbles" morally when another Jew sins.

The Gemorah therefore says that every Jew is an Arev for every other Jew. We have loosely translated the word Arev as "responsible," but in a more precise sense, it means "surety" or a "cosigner."

In order to understand this, let us look at the example implied by this term. Suppose that you want me to lend you money, but I am not sure that you will be able to repay it. What can you do? One thing would be to call a friend and ask him to be a cosigner (Arev) for your loan. Then, if you cannot repay it your cosigner is responsible.

In accepting the Torah, every Jew took upon himself a certain responsibility to observe it. But he also took upon himself the responsibility to be a "cosigner" (Arev) for every other Jew. Therefore, if any Jew does not pay his "debt" to God, every other Jew in the world bears a measure of responsibility for it.

This has important implications in Jewish law. Thus, for example, there is a rule that you can say a blessing for another person. In general, however, this is only true when you yourself have an obligation to say the blessing. Since you are fulfilling your own obligation, you can, at the same time, do so for another person.

Thus, for example, if you are eating together with another person, and for some reason he cannot say the blessing, then you can say it for him. All that he must do is have in mind that he is being included in your blessing, and if possible, answer Amen. This is only true, however, if you are eating with him. If you do not eat, you yourself do not have an obligation, and you therefore cannot say the blessing for another person.[9]

In the case of the blessing over a commandment, however, this is not the case. There, you can say the blessing for another person, even if you have already fulfilled your own obligation. The Ran (Rabenu Nissim) gives a very pertinent reason for this. He quotes the teaching that every Jew is responsible as a "cosigner" for the observance of every other Jew. Therefore, even if you yourself have fulfilled your obligation, as long as another Jew has not fulfilled it, your fulfillment is also not complete. Since your fulfillment is not complete, you are also included in the blessing that you are saying for the other person (see readings).

The classic case where we see such mutual responsibility is in the case of Achan. When Joshua conquered Jericho, he dedicated all the spoil to God. Achan, however, violated this dedication, and took a few things from the spoil for himself. As he himself later was to confess (*Joshua 7:21*), "I saw in the spoil a nice Shinar mantle, two hundred silver shekels, and a golden wedge weighing fifty shekels. I coveted them and took them, and they are hidden in the ground in the middle of my tent."

Even though only a single person had sinned, the Scripture says (*Ibid., 7:1*), "The children of Israel committed a sin with regard to the devoted spoil. For Achan . . . took the devoted thing, and God's anger was kindled against Israel." As a result of this single individual's misdeed, God's protection was taken away from all Israel, and they suffered their first defeat after having crossed the Jordan, in the battle of Ai. Only one person had sinned, but it had an effect on every Jew. Joshua was later to declare (*Ibid., 22:20*), "Did not Achan, the son of Zerah, commit a sin with the devoted spoil, and as a result, wrath fell upon the entire congregation of Israel? He did not perish alone for his sin."

In the Midrash (see readings), Rabbi Shimon bar Yochai provides us with a very good example. He likens all Israel to the passengers on a single huge ship. Every time a person sins, he is like one who drills a hole in the ship. Even though others may be very careful not to damage the hull, if the hole causes the ship to sink, all will drown. The main point is that all Jews are in the same boat, and whenever any Jew does not keep the Torah, all are ultimately affected.

We can also understand all this on a deeper level. One of the concepts of Judaism is the imitation of God.[10] The Gemorah tells us that we must imitate God in all His attributes, showing kindness, mercy and charity to all.[11] When we imitate God, we draw close to Him spiritually, and thus become worthy of "basking in the glow of the Divine Presence."[12]

There is one attribute of God, however, that would appear very difficult to imitate. This is His unity. Our most basic declaration of faith is that "HaShem is our God, HaShem is One"—and this speaks of the most fundamental attribute of God that has been revealed to us. But if we are to imitate God, how can we imitate His attribute of Unity?

We can find an answer in one of the most mystical teachings of the Gemorah, which speaks of God's Tefillin.[13] Of course, a detailed discussion of this concept is beyond the scope of this book and has already been discussed in another work.[14] But what is important to our discussion is the parallel that the Gemorah draws between the Tefillin that we wear and God's Tefillin.

As we all know, one of the most important parchments in our Tefillin is that which contains the Sh'ma, "Hear O Israel, HaShem is our God. HaShem is One." The Gemorah tells us that God's Tefillin also contains a "parchment." In this "parchment" is a parallel to the Sh'ma (1 Chronicles 17:21), "Who is like Your people Israel, *a nation one on earth*, whom God went to redeem for Himself as a people, to make Himself a name by great and tremendous things."

This parallel answers our question. The way in which we imitate God's unity is by being "a nation one on earth"—by being unified and together as a people. The closer together and more unified the Jewish people become, the more they as a whole resemble God.

We therefore see that the only way in which we can imitate God's most important revealed attribute is by acting as a single unity. This explains why this unity is stressed so often in Jewish literature. It also explains why we accepted the Torah as a unified whole, and why we have the mutual responsibility for its observance.

On a more mystical level, the entire Jewish people can be looked upon as a single organic whole—like a great body encompassing all of its individuals.[15] If any part of the body is infected, or if poison is injected into even a single extremity, then the individual as a whole suffers, and every other part of the body is also affected. The same is true of the Jewish people. If even a single Jew does not keep the Torah, all of us suffer.

On Yom Kippur, when we ask God to forgive our sins we also confess all of our wrongdoings to Him. It is interesting to note, however, that we do not say "I have sinned," but "we have sinned." The codes also tell us that we should pray the confession even for sins that we ourselves may have never committed. The reason for all of this is because as long as even a single Jew has committed this sin, all of us are responsible.[16]

The Gemorah tells us that this responsibility for the sins of others exists primarily when we do not do anything to try to prevent them from doing wrong. When a person has the opportunity to bring others to the right path, and does not take advantage of this opportunity, then he bears complete responsibility for the other's wrongdoing. This shall be discussed in more detail in Chapter Four.

NOTES

1. *Rosh HaShanah* 17a; *Yad. Tshuva* 3:11, *Avel* 1:10; *Shulchan Aruch, Yoreh Deah* 345:5, 340:4 in *Hagah.*
2. *Shaarey Tshuvah* 3:168.
3. *Shavuos* 29a, *Nedarim* 25a. Also see *Nedarim* 8a, *Nazir* 4a: *Yad, Nedarim* 3:7, *Shavuos* 11:3; *Sifsey Cohen, Yoreh Deah* 119:22, *Tshuvos Nodeh BeYehudah, Orech Chaim* 1:38, *Tshuvos Shaagas Aryeh* 60, Maharitz Chayos *Nedarim* 8a, *Nazir* 4a, *Tshuvos Rambam* 170.
4. *Yoreh Deah* 218:35.
5. *Ibid.*, Maharsha, *Shavuos* 29a "*HeSheHishbia,*" Rashash *ibid.*, HaGra; *Yoreh Deah* 228:99, *Tshuvos HaRosh* 5:4, *Tshuvos Rivash* 399.
6. Rashi, Rambam *ad loc.* See *Shavuos* 36a, where we find that the expression "cursed" also indicates an oath, and this is derived from this verse. Also see Yad, *Shavuos* 2:2.
7. *Yerushalmi, Sotah* 7:4 (31a), Ramban on Deuteronomy 27:26.
8. This answers the question raised by the *Minchas Chinuch* 232:4. See *Zohar* 3:85a, *Minchas Pittim, Orech Chaim* 156, *Makor Chesed* (on *Sefer Chasidim*) 673:1. Also Rambam, *Tosefos Yom Tov,* on *Shevi'is* 5:6.
9. *Magen Avraham* 167:40, *Mishnah Berurah* 167:92.
10. *Derech HaShem* 1:2:1.

11. *Sotah* 14a, *Yad, Deyos* 1:8.
12. *Berachos* 17a, *Yad Tshuvah* 8:2.
13. *Berachos* 6a.
14. See *God, Man and Tefillin* (NCSY, New York, 1973), p. 33 ff.
15. *Kuzari* 3:19, *Zohar* 3:218a, *Derech Mitzvosecha, Mitzvas Ahavas Yisroel* p. 28a.
16. *Turay Zahav, Orech Chaim* 607:1.

READINGS

———◆———

TALMUD

In the case of every other sin in the Torah, (only) the individual himself is punished. But here (in the case of a false oath), both he and the entire world are punished.

And in the case of all the sins in the Torah the entire world is not punished? (This seems to be a contradiction.)

It is written (*Leviticus 26:27*), "A man shall stumble for his brother." (This means that each man shall stumble morally) because of the sin of his brother. From this we learn that all Israel are responsible, one for the other.

This (latter) case is speaking where one has the opportunity to protest and does not do so.

Shavuos 39a

Ahavah, the son of Rabbi Zeira taught: With respect to all blessings, even if one has already fulfilled his own obligation, he (can say the blessing for another person and thus) can fulfill the obligation of another.

Rosh HaShana 29a (bottom)

(The reason for this is) because "all Israel are responsible, one for the other" with regard to (the observance of the) command-ments.

Rashi ad loc

This is because "all Israel are responsible, one for the other" with regard to (the observance of the) commandments. Therefore, as long as another person has not fulfilled his obligation, it is the same as if he himself had not fulfilled it.

Ran (Rabenu Nissim) ad loc

---◆---

MECHILTA

(The Mechilta is the oldest Talmudical commentary on the Book of Exodus)

It is written *(Jeremiah 3:17)*, "Israel is a scattered sheep, lions (have driven her away)." (Israel) is likened to a sheep. When a sheep is struck in one of her limbs, all of her limbs feel it. The same is true of Israel: One person sins, and all are punished.

Mechilta on Exodus 19:6

---◆---

MIDRASH

Hezekiah discussed the verse *(Jeremiah 3:17)*, "Israel is a scat-tered sheep."

Why is Israel likened to a sheep? When a sheep is struck on the head or on any other limb, all of her limbs feel it. The same is true of Israel: One individual sins, and they all feel it. It is thus written *(Numbers 16:22)*, "One man sins, (and You become angry at the entire congregation)."

Rabbi Shimon bar Yochai gave an example. A number of people were sitting in a ship. One of them took a drill and began making holes in the hull. The others asked him, "What do you think you're doing?"

The driller replied, "What business is it of yours? I am only drilling under my own seat."

They answered, "When water fills the ship, it will sink with all of us."

VaYikra Rabbah 4:6

You may ask, why were 42,000 people killed in the time of Jephthah? Jephthah had made an incorrect vow, and Pinchas, son of Eliezer, was still alive at the time. Jephthah should have gone to Pinchas to have his vow annulled, but he did not do so. He said, "I am the leader of all Israel, should I then go to *him?*" Pinchas, on the other hand, also said, "He needs me. Should I then go to *him?*" . . .

All the people of Ephraim then came (to Jephthah) to start a fight with him. Pinchas should have spoken up and said, "You have not come to Jephthah to annul his vow. You have come to start a war." It is bad enough that Pinchas did not protest what the people of Ephraim did, but he also did not annul Jephthah's vow.

But God who sits on His throne is a righteous judge—let His great Name be blessed for ever and ever. He said, "Jephthah placed his life in his hands to save Israel from Moab and Ammon, and now these people are coming to start a great fight with him? *They* are going to wage war with him?" Jephthah was therefore able to go out and kill 42,000 people.

It is thus written (*Judges 12:1–6*):

The men of Ephraim gathered together . . . and they said to Jephthah, "Why did you go over to fight against the people of Ammon and not call us (to go with you)? We will burn your house around you with fire."

And Jephthah said, "I and my people were having great

strife (with the people of Ammon. But when I called you, you did nothing to save me). When I saw that you were not helping me, I took my life in my hands (and crossed over against the children of Ammon. God then delivered them into my hand.) Why then do you come now to fight aginst me?"

Then Jephthah gathered together all the men of Gilead, and fought against Ephraim. . . . They caught them and killed them at the fords of the Jordan. At that time, 42,000 men of Ephraim fell.

Who killed all these people? We must say that it was Pinchas, since he had the opportunity to protest, and did not do so. . . .

This is not only true of Pinchas. Every person who has the ability to protest and does not do so—or who can bring Israel back to doing good and does not do so—is held responsible for all the blood that is spilled among the Jews. It is thus written (*Ezekiel 3:17, 18*), "I have appointed you as a sentry for the house of Israel. When you hear a word from Me, warn them in My name. When I say to a wicked man, 'You must die,' and you do not warn him . . . then that wicked man shall die with his sin, but I will seek his blood from your hands." For "all Israel are responsible, one for the other."

What is this like? When a single cabin is torn open in a ship, one does not say that "a cabin has been torn open," but that "the ship has been torn open."

The same is true of Israel. It is thus written (*Joshua 22:20*), "Did not Achan, son of Zerah, take the forbidden things, and as a result, wrath fell upon the entire congregation of Israel? He was just one man, but he did not perish (alone) for his sin."

You may ask, why were 70,000 people killed in Givat Binyamin?

The great Sanhedrins, founded by Moses, Joshua and Pinchas, were in existence at that time. They should have tied iron thongs around their waists and lifted their robes above their knees. Then they should have gone around to all the cities of Israel, one day to Lachish, one day to Bethel, one day to Jerusalem, until they visited all the cities in Israel. They could have taught all Israel proper conduct in one, two or three years, and Israel would have settled their land properly. God's name would have then been made great and holy in all the worlds that He created, from one end of the universe to the other.

They did not do this, however. Each one went to his own land and to his own vineyard. He enjoyed his wine and his field, and said, "My soul shall be at peace." They did not wish to exert themselves. . . .

As a result, Torah and proper conduct did not exist in Givat Binyamin. They therefore went to war, and 70,000 people were killed. But who killed them all? We must say that it was the great Sanhedrins, established by Moses, Joshua and Pinchas.

Tana DeBei Eliahu Rabbah 11

———◆———

RABBI YEHUDAH HA-CHASID: SEFER CHASIDIM

"All Israel are responsible, one for the other." It is thus written (*Exodus 24:3*), "And all the people answered *with a single voice*, and said, 'All the words that God speaks, we will obey.'" If even a single individual would have protested, the Torah would not have been given.

It is for this reason that we say (in the prayer *Sim Shalom* in the *Amidah*), "Bless us, our Father, *all of us as one*, with the light of Your countenance, (for in the light of Your countenance, You gave us the Torah of life)."

Sefer Chasidim 233

It is written (*Daniel 9:15*), "We have sinned, we have been wicked." (Daniel) included himself among the sinners because "all Israel are responsible, one for the other."

With regard to Achan (who violated Joshua's ban), it is written (*Joshua 22:20*), "(Did not Achan, son of Zerah, commit a sin with the devoted thing, and as a result, wrath fell upon the entire congregation of Israel?) He was just one man, but he did not perish (alone) for his sin."

Therefore, when we say the confession (in the *Amidah*), we say it in the plural form, "Forgive *us* our Father for *we* have sinned." Similarly, when we confess (on Yom Kippur), we say, "for the sins which carry a penalty of stoning, burning, sword and strangulation." This is even said by individuals who know for certain that they have never committed such a sin. The reason for this is because "all Israel are responsible, one for the other."

Sefer Chasidim 601

———◆———

RABBI ELIAHU DI VIDASH: RESHIS CHOCHMAH

It is written (*Deuteronomy 32:9*), "(For His people are a portion of God), Jacob the rope of His inheritance." This indicates that all Jewish souls are bound to one another like a plaited rope, and are therefore united together with no separation.

When you shake one end of a taut rope, the entire rope vibrates. This is the meaning of the verse (*Numbers 16:22*), "One man sins, and You rage at the entire congregation." This also explains the case of Achan. The reason for all this is because "all Israel are responsible, one for the other."

Reshis Chochmah, Shaar HaYirah 14

———◆———

RABBI YEHUDAH HA-LEVI: KUZARI

When a person separates himself from the community, thinking that he will remain alone, he wrongs the community as a whole, but he actually wrongs himself still more. In relation to the community as a whole, each individual is like a limb of the body.

If the arm were not to allow itself (to receive an injection of) medication, it would harm the entire body. The arm itself, however, would also share in this injury.

Kuzari 3:19

---◆---

RABBI YITZCHOK LURIA (THE ARI)

The Commandment *(Leviticus 19:18):* "You shall love your neighbor as yourself."

You must realize that all Israel form a mysterious single body, consisting of Adam's soul. This is the mystery of the verse *(Ecclesiastes 8:9),* "the time when Adam dominates over man." Every single Jew is like an individual limb (of this mystical body).

This is the (reason for the) responsibility that every Jew bears for every other Jew who sins.

It is for this reason that my master (the Ari) would say every confession (in the service), even for sins that he had never committed. He said, "Even though a person may have never committed a sin, he must (ask God to forgive him for it) and confess it." It is for this reason that the wording of the confession is in the plural—"we have sinned"—and not "I have sinned."

The reason for this is because all the Jews (collectively) form a single body. Therefore, even if an individual has never committed a particular sin, he should confess it anyway. For if another Jew has committed this sin, it is the same as if he himself had done so. It is also for this reason that the confession is written in the plural.

When a person prays (for forgiveness) and says the confession, even at home alone, he must therefore say ("we have sinned") in the plural. For as a result of the connection between all souls, when any Jew sins, it is counted as if all Israel participated in that sin.

Likutey Torah, Taamey HaMitzvos on Leviticus 19:18.

III

The Commandment

U p until now, we have discussed our responsibility toward other Jews primarily in terms of our moral obligations. Besides this, however, there is actually a commandment in the Torah that obligates us to speak up when we see others doing wrong, and to do everything in our power to bring them back to the right path.

The Torah states (*Leviticus 19:17*), "You shall not hate your brother in your heart, you must correct your neighbor, and do not bear a sin because of him." The statement, "You must correct your neighbor," is counted as one of the 613 commandments of the Torah, and it gives every Jew the obligation to correct any other Jew who is doing wrong."

The exact Hebrew wording in the Torah is *Hokheach Tokh-iach*—literally, "Correct, you shall correct." The double wording strengthens the phrase and indicates that this is something that we *must* do, and not merely moral advice. It is for this reason that we loosely translate the phrase as "you must correct." From the double wording, the Gemorah derives a number of rules, and these are quoted in the readings at the end of this chapter.

As a commandment of the Torah, this obligation is the subject of a somewhat extensive body of Jewish Law. We will outline some aspects of it here, and present a more detailed outline in the last chapter.

Most English translations render the word *Hokheach* as "admonish" or "rebuke." This, however, is not a precise translation. The words "admonish" or "rebuke" have the connotation that one should "tell off" the person doing wrong, speaking to him in a harsh, stern manner. It is for this reason that we translate the word as "correct." As most authorities explain, the best way to fulfill this commandment and "correct" another person is not with harsh words, but by drawing him to God with love and affection.

This is actually born out by experience. If you want to bring somebody back to the true path, the worst possible thing that you can do is to berate him, and to "admonish" or "rebuke" him. If you want to have any chance of success, the best way is to be as pleasant and friendly as possible, drawing the person with words of love, and gradually strengthening him spiritually. Indeed, the best way to fulfill this commandment would be to follow the advice of Hillel, who said, "love people and bring them to the Torah."[2] As the commentaries point out, this was the way of Aaron. If he saw a person sinning, he would befriend him and speak to him, until the person himself realized that he was doing wrong, and thus corrected himself.[3]

We actually see this from the context of the commandment. The Torah says, "You shall not hate your brother in your heart, you must correct your neighbor." What the Torah is essentially saying is that when you correct a person, you may not have any hatred whatsoever, even in your heart. The best way to correct another person is with the deepest expression of love.[4]

On another level, we may think that if a person does not keep the Torah, then we should have nothing at all to do with him. This, however, is equivalent to hatred. As our sages teach us, being indifferent and not speaking to a person is in itself an

expression of hatred—or at least, of the lack of love.⁵ But the
Torah tells us that if we see a person doing wrong, we should not
hate him "in our heart," but should speak out to correct him, and
do our best to bring him back to the path of life. The Torah
therefore says, "You shall not hate your brother in your heart, you
must correct your neighbor."⁶

According to a number of authorities, the word *hoKheaCh*
(correct) comes from the same root as *noKhaCh,* meaning "opposite."⁷ In this sense, it means confronting a person with his
wrongdoing, and doing everything in one's power to correct it.

In a deeper sense, however, it can also mean that you should
confront a person with himself. You must bring a person to
confront the human situation, and make him ask why he was
born and why he is living. You must make him realize how much
God loves every individual, and how this bond of love is fulfilled
through the Torah. When a person confronts himself in this
manner, he will have no choice but to return to the right path.

In many places, the word *hoKheaCh* also means to prove
something. Here, however, the Torah is not telling us to prove
something *to* someone else, but to prove *him*—that is, to show
him what he truly is. Here again, we can take a cue from Rabbi
Levi Yitzchok, who says that the best way to correct a person is to
convince him of his own spiritual worth, and how important his
deeds are in God's eyes (see readings).

Rabbi Samson Raphael Hirsch (quoted in a later section) states
that the word *hoKheaCh* is also phono-semantically related to the
word *Yaga,* which means to make a person think. For what are we
doing when we make a person confront himself, if not making him
think? Usually when a person does wrong, it is because he is not
aware of the truth, or because he does not wish to think about
it—as the Gemorah says, "he has in him a spirit of foolishness."⁸
If we are successful in making a person think, then he will correct
his ways on his own.

Other authorities state that the word *hoKheaCh* shares the
same root with the word *KoaCh,* meaning strength.⁹ According
to this, the main connotation of this word is that one should
strengthen another person both morally and spiritually. As long as
a person is doing wrong and not following the right path, he is
weak in this respect. We are commanded to strengthen him.

In expressing this commandment, the Torah says, "You must correct your neighbor, and do not bear a sin because of him." This has two connotations. One is expressed in the Gemorah, and that is, you should not sin while correcting another. This means that you should not do it in a manner that will in any way embarrass him, since embarrassing another person is considered a most serious sin[10] (see readings).

From this, it is obvious that when we correct others, we must do so with the utmost tact and thoughtfulness. If you correct another person in an embarrassing manner, rather than fulfilling a Mitzvah, you are committing a most serious sin.

The second connotation is that if you do not correct your friend, doing everything in your power to improve him, then you are responsible for all of his wrongdoings. If you do not "correct your neighbor," then you will indeed "bear a sin because of him."[11] This is closely related to the concept of mutual responsibility that is discussed in the previous and following chapters.

From all this, we see that when people all around us do not keep the Torah, we certainly have an obligation to speak up and do whatever we can to remedy the situation. But still, there are limitations. One, which we have already discussed, is that this must be done lovingly and tactfully. This, as we have already seen, is an integral part of the commandment.

Besides this, there must be some chance that your word and deeds will have some effect. As long as there is even the remotest chance that you can do some good, you have the obligation to speak out. There are many instances, however, in which you know for certain that your words will have no effect. In such cases, the obligation no longer exists. As the author of the *Torah Temimah* explains, the very word "correct" indicates that your words will at least have a chance of producing some effect. Where no such chance exists, there is no longer any obligation.[12] Regarding such cases, our sages say, "Just as it is a Mitzvah to say something that will be accepted, so it is a Mitzvah not to say something when it will not be accepted" (see readings). The precise conditions will be discussed in more detail in the last section.

The Torah furthermore says that, "you must correct your neighbor (*Amis-echa*)." In a number of places, the Gemorah says that a person is not considered "your neighbor" (Amis-echa) unless he is "with you in Torah and Mitzvos."[13] Indeed, the word used for friend here (Amis), shares the same root with the word Umas, meaning "parallel" or "counterpart."[14] The obligation is therefore primarily directed at those who can be considered "your neighbor" and excludes those who are so far from the true path that there is absolutely no chance that they will accept any moral or religious correction.

These two concepts are actually very closely related. If a person is "your neighbor," then there is also a chance that he will listen to you. If, on the other hand, he is so far from the Torah that he is not "your neighbor," then this means that you are also certain that he will not accept anything that you tell him. In such a case, this commandment no longer obligates you to even try to improve him; the Torah does not require us to engage in futile tasks. If there is any chance that he might be improved, however, then he is still considered "your neighbor," and you have every obligation to do whatever you can to bring him back to the right path.[15]

Under certain conditions, our sages also teach us that we should not correct others, because "it is better that they sin unknowingly, and not sin knowingly" (see readings). Many people take this saying and use it as an excuse to not even try to bring irreligious Jews back to their heritage. But actually, when we look into the context of this statement, as well as into what the codes say about it, we see that it only applies under very specific conditions.

Unless the following conditions are true, we have an obligation to speak out—even if it will bring people to sin knowingly rather than unknowingly:

1. The transgression must involve a commandment that is not mentioned expressly in the Torah. Where something is mentioned in the Torah, we must speak out in all cases.
2. It must be practiced habitually.
3. The people doing it must not realize that they are doing wrong. If they realize that what they are doing is wrong, one must correct them under all conditions.

4. It must be certain that they will not be improved if they are told that they are wrong. If there is any chance that one will effectively deter them, he must speak out.

Only when these four conditions are fulfilled do we say that "it is better that they sin unknowingly." In every other case, one has the obligation to speak out and do everything in his power. (See excerpt from Hirsch, and section on Laws.)

Even this exception, however, may not apply in our time. The Ritva (Rabbi Yom Tov ben Avraham), one of the foremost early authorities (*Rishonim*), states that the exemption that "they not sin knowingly" only applies in a time when people are generally observant, but in a few isolated instances, people are ignorant of their obligations. In a time when people might forget the entire Torah out of ignorance, however, one must do everything in one's power to do whatever he can to remedy the situation (see readings).

In general, we therefore see that this commandment places a very strong obligation on every faithful Jew in our generation. As we shall see in a later section, the Chafetz Chaim (Rabbi Yisroel Meir HaCohen) spoke out most strongly about this obligation more than seventy years ago. But what was a minor blaze in his generation, has become a conflagration in ours. No religious Jew today can absolve himself from this responsibility.

NOTES

1. *Yad, Deyos* 6:7, *Sefer HaMitzvos*, positive 205, *Sefer Mitzvos Gadol (Smag)*, positive 11, *Sefer Yereyim* 223, *Sefer Mitzvos Katan (Smak)* 112, *Sefer HaChinuch* 239, *Cheredim* 4:28.
2. *Avos* 1:12.
3. Rambam, Bertenoro, Rabenu Yonah, *ad loc., Avos DeRabbi Nathan* 12:3.
4. *Kli Yakar ad loc.*.
5. *Sanhedrin* 3:5 (27b), *Yad, Rozeach* 6:10, *Choshen Mishpat* 7:7 *in Hagah.*
6. See *Paneach Raza ad loc. Cf. Hagahos Maimoni on Yad, Deyos* 6:3, *Chazon Ish, Ibid.*
7. *HaKesav VeHaKaballah ad loc. Cf. Ibn Ezra* on Genesis 20:16.
8. *Sotah* 3a, *BaMidbar Rabbah* 9:3 *Cf.* Proverbs 3:32, 9:16.
9. See *Aruch* "Koach."

10. *Avos* 3:11, *Baba Metzia* 99a, 107a; *Yad, Tshuvah* 3:14, *Deyos* 6:8, *Shaarey Tshuvah* 3:141.
11. *Or HaChaim, Kli Yakar, Nachal Kadomim* (Chida) *ad loc., Sefer Chasidim* 5.
12. *Torah Temimah ad loc.* 114. See Rashi, *Yebamos* 65b *"Lomar."*
13. *Baba Metzia* 58b, *Shavuos* 30a.
14. Radak, *Sefer HaSherashim "Amas."* Ibn Ezra, Malbim on Numbers 5:21. *Cf.* Rashi on Zechariah 13:7.
15. *Minchas Chinuch* 239:4.

READINGS

———◆———

TALMUD

One of the rabbis said to Rava, "Can we assume that 'correct' (*HoKheaCh*) means (that you must correct your neighbor) once, and that 'you shall correct' (*ToKhiaCh*) means twice?"

(Rava) replied, "Correct (*HoKheaCh*) means even a hundred times."

(What then do we learn from the expression) "You shall correct?"

(If the Torah would have only said 'correct') we would only know that a teacher must correct his student. How do we know that even a student must correct his teacher? The Torah therefore says. "Correct, you shall correct" (*HoKheach ToKhiach*), (which includes) every case.

Baba Metzia 31a

How do we know that if you see another person doing wrong that you must correct him? It is written, "Correct, you shall correct (your neighbor)."

If you correct him and he does not accept it, how do we know that you must try again? It is written, "You shall correct." (This includes every case.)

We might think that (this is true) even if his face changes color. It is therefore written, "You shall not bear a sin because of him."

A teaching (from the time of the Mishnah):

Rabbi Tarfon said, "I would be very surprised if there is anyone in this generation who can accept correction. If you tell someone, 'Why don't you remove that splinter from between your teeth,' he replies. 'Why don't you take that tree trunk out of your own eye!'"

Rabbi Elazar ben Azariah said, "I would be very surprised if there is anyone in this generation who knows how to correct another."

Rabbi Yochanan ben Nuri said, "Heaven and earth can bear witness that Rabbi Akiva was struck many times because of me when I complained about him to Rabban Gamaliel. But this caused him to love me all the more. This was a fulfillment of the scripture (Proverbs 9:8), 'Do not correct a scoffer, lest he hate you—correct the wise man, and he will love you.'"

(The students) asked Rabbi Yehudah, the son of Rabbi Shimon, "(When a person's own personal injury is involved) what is better, to correct the other person for the sake (of God), or to be humble (and not say anything), not for the sake (of God)?"

He replied, "Do you not agree that humility is the best trait? Even if not meant for the sake (of God), it is still the better course. . . ."

What is an example of correcting another for the sake (of God), and being humble, not for the sake (of God)?

(An example is) the case of Rav Huna and Chiyah, son of Rav. They were both disciples of Shmuel. Chiyah, the son of Rav, said to (Shmuel), "Master, see how Rav Hunah is making me suffer." Rav Hunah (did not reply but) accepted upon himself that he would no longer do anything to hurt (Chiyah).

After (Chiyah, son of Rav) left, (Rav Hunah) told (Shmuel), "These are the (terrible) things that (Chiyah) did to me, (and therefore, I had to retaliate to make him stop)."

(Shmuel) asked, "Why didn't you say something to me in his presence?"

(Rav Hunah) replied, "Heaven forbid that a child of Rav should be shamed because of me."

Until when does one have the obligations to correct (another)?

Rav says, "Until he strikes back physically!" Shmuel says, "Until (he replies with) a curse." Ben Azai said, "Until he displays anger."

It is like (an earlier dispute between) Tana'im (Rabbis of the Mishnah): Rabbi Eliezer said, "Until he strikes back physically." Rabbi Joshua said. "Until (he replies with) a curse." Ben Azai said, "Until he displays anger."

Rav Nachman bar Yitzchok said: All three derive this from the same scripture. (After Jonathan had tried to convince King Saul that he was behaving wrongly toward David) we find (*I Samuel 20:30*), "Saul's anger was kindled against Jonathan, and he said to him. 'You son of perverse rebellion—you have chosen the son of Jesse to your own shame, and to the shame of your mother's nakedness.'" It is then written (*Ibid., 20:33*). "And Saul cast his spear at him to strike him."

The one who says, "Until he strikes back physically," (derives this from the fact that) it is written, "to strike him."

The one who says, "Until (he replies with) a curse," (derives it from the fact that) it is written. "(You son of perverse rebellion . . .) to your own shame, and to the shame of your mother's nakedness."

The one who says, "Until he displays anger," (derives it from the fact that) it is written, "Saul's anger was kindled against Jonathan."

According to the opinion that says, "Until he displays anger," (why do we find) a curse and a blow (also mentioned) in the scripture? Jonathan loved David so much, he was willing to (go beyond what was required and) endanger his life for him.

Arachin 16b

Rabbi Ila'a said in the name of Rabbi Elazar, son of Rabbi Shimon: Just like it is a Mitzvah to say something that will be accepted, so is it a Mitzvah not to say something that will not be accepted.

Rabbi Abba said: It is an obligation (to remain silent in such a case). It is thus written (*Proverbs 9:8*), "Do not correct a scoffer, lest he hate you; correct the wise man, and he will love you."

Yebamos 65b

(It is a Mitzvah to speak out when it will be accepted) as it is written, "You must correct (your neighbor." However, this only refers to) one who will accept (correction).

Rashi ad loc.

———◆———

MIDRASH

"You must correct your neighbor." One might think that you must even correct a wicked person who will hate you (for doing so). It is therefore written, "You must correct *your neighbor*"— you must only correct "your neighbor" who is close to you in Torah and Mitzvos, and who will love you (when you correct him). A wicked person, on the other hand, will hate you, and therefore, you have no obligation to correct him—neither are you permitted to do so.

Tanna DeBei Eliahu Rabbah 18

———◆———

RAMBAM (MAIMONIDES)

A person who sees his friend sinning or going in the wrong way has an obligation to bring him back and improve him, explaining that he is harming himself with his evil deeds. It is thus written, "You must correct your neighbor."

When you correct your friend, whether with regard to personal matters or with regard to his relationship with God, you must do so privately. You should speak to him calmly and in a gentle voice, telling him that you are only speaking to him for his own good, to bring him to life in the World to Come.

If he accepts what you say, good. If not, you must correct him again, two and three times. You have the obligation to continue correcting your friend until he (actually) strikes you and says, "I will not listen."

Whoever has the opportunity to protest (wrongdoing) and does not do so, is caught up in the sin, since he was able to protest against their (actions).

Yad, Deyos 6:7

We are commanded to correct a person who is sinning, or who (even) wishes to sin, and prevent him from doing so. We must speak up and correct him. (This is the commandment, "You must correct your neighbor.")

It is not proper to say, "I am not sinning. If another person sins, what business is it of mine?" Such an attitude goes against the Torah.

We ourselves are commanded not to sin, and (we are also commanded) not to allow any one else of our faith to rebel. If he continues to rebel, then we must correct him and bring him back. This is true even when there are no witnesses and he has not been brought to court (for his misdeeds).

This is what God meant when He said, "You must correct your neighbor."

In the words of the *Sifri*: How do we know that if you correct another two or three times, that you must still continue doing so? It is written "Correct, you shall correct"—(which means) even a thousand times. One may think that you must correct him (in such a manner) that his face changes color. The Torah says, "You shall not bear a sin because of him."

Our sages explain that this commandment obligates every person. Even the lowliest (must correct) those of high status.

Even if (the person you are correcting) curses you and insults you, you should not desist until he threatens (you physically).

Those who accepted the Torah said, "(You must continue correcting another) until he strikes back physically."

Sefer HaMitzvos 205

———◆———

RABBI ELIAHU: THE VILNA GAON

One of our sages said, "I would be very surprised if there is anyone in this generation who knows how to correct another." For there are two ways of correcting others. When you correct someone with harsh words and shame him, saying, "Why did you do this?" you insult him, and he will not listen to you. The Tzadik (righteous person), however, comes with pleasant, gentle words, and draws a person to the Torah. Everybody then wants to follow this Tzadik. It is thus said of Aaron *(Avos 1:12),* "He loved peace, pursued peace, loved people and drew them to the Torah."

Commentary on Proverbs 10:20

———◆———

RABBI LEVI YITZCHOK OF BERDICHOV

There are two ways in which one can correct other Jews and bring them to follow the Creator's will.

One way is to correct them with pleasant words. You can explain to every Jew how important he is, and how lofty is his soul—since all Jewish souls are actually hewn from a place higher than the Throne of Glory. You can tell them of the great pleasure that God has from the Mitzvos kept by each individual Jew, and of the great joy that exists in all the (spiritual) worlds when even a single Jew observes God's commandments.

In this manner, you can influence Jewish hearts to do God's will. You can cause every individual Jew to accept upon himself the Yoke of the Heavenly Kingdom.

The other way is to correct people with harsh words, using phrases calculated to shame them into fulfilling God's will. There is a great difference between this and the previous way.

One who corrects other Jews by speaking of their greatness uplifts Jewish souls higher and higher. He constantly speaks of Israel's righteousness and greatness, telling how great their strength is on high. Such an individual is worthy of being a leader. This, however, is not true of one who corrects them with harsh words.

Kedushas Levi, Chukas

◆

THE CODES

Leave Israel alone, it is better that they sin unknowingly, and not sin knowingly.

Talmud: Betza 30a

This is only speaking of a case where we are certain that they are doing it unknowingly. In such a case, we are not "caught up in their sin" when (it is certain) that it would not help if we spoke up.

In a case where we know that they realize that they are doing wrong, this reason is no longer valid. Therefore, if we do not speak up, we are "caught up in their sin," since "(all) Israel are responsible, one for the other."

. . . When the Gemorah says that (it is better that they sin unknowingly, and) we need not speak up even in the case of a Torah law, it is not speaking of a law actually written in the Torah. Rather (as in the case under discussion), it is speaking of something that is derived logically from the scripture. (In the case of a law that is actually written in the Torah, however, one must speak out in all cases.)

. . . The Ritva (Rabbi Yom Tov ben Avraham) quotes a great

Ashkenazic rabbi, who testifies in the name of the rabbis of France, including Rabenu Yitzchok and Rabbi Meir of Rothenberg, saying that this was only true in their generations. But in this generation, where people are lax regarding many laws, we must "make a fence around the Torah." Therefore, even where Rabbinical law is concerned, one must speak up . . . so that they should not sin, either knowingly or unknowingly. . . . This opinion seems to be correct.

Furthermore, even in their times, the only instance where they did not speak out was when they were absolutely certain that their words would not be accepted. If there is any chance that it might be accepted, however, one must certainly speak up. We see this from the Gemorah (*Shabbos 55a*).

Shitah Mekubetzes ad loc.

This only applies to a law not written explicitly in the Torah. . . . But when a law is written explicitly in the Torah, one must protest in every case.

Rabbi Asher (Rosh) ad loc.

The same rule applies to every prohibition, and we say that, "It is better that they sin unknowingly, and not sin knowingly." (Therefore, one should not speak out.)

This is true, however, only of such laws that are not stated explicitly in the Torah, even if they are Torah laws (*DeOraisa*). But where a law is stated explicitly in the Torah, one must speak out.

If you know that people will not listen to you, you should not speak out publicly to correct them. You should only (speak out) once, but you should not correct them many times, since you know that they will not listen to you.

Where an individual is concerned, however, you have the obligation (to speak out and) correct him, until he strikes you or curses you.

Shulchan Aruch, Orach Chaim 608:2 in Hagah

IV
Mutual Responsibility

*T*he commandment discussed in the previous chapter gives us a most important obligation. If we see others not living by the Torah, then we must do whatever we can to correct the situation. If we do not do so, then we ourselves are responsible for whatever wrong they do.

In one place, the Chafetz Chaim (Rabbi Yisroel Meir Ha-Cohen) gives a very good example. He tells us that a person may keep kosher in the strictest possible manner all his life. He may examine the certification of every thing that enters his mouth, and abstain from anything whose Kashrus is even slightly questionable. Yet, when he ultimately stands in judgement before God, he will be asked, "Why did you eat pork?" This person will protest that he never let even the smallest speck of swine flesh pass his lips. But then he will be told, "You knew that other Jews were eating pork. Why did you do nothing about it?"[1]

The Gemorah teaches us that anyone who can prevent others

from doing wrong and does not do so, is held responsible for their sins (see readings). If you can influence a friend to live by the Torah, then you have the responsibility to do so. If you can influence the members of your family, then you have the responsibility to do so. If there is any way in the world that you can go out and bring others to the truth, then you have the responsibility to do so.

You have this responsibility even if you are not sure that you will do any good. We see this in the Gemorah. God had said that He Himself was certain that if the righteous of Jerusalem had spoken up, it would not have done any good. The Attribute of Justice, however, was still able to successfully argue that, "If it was known to You, was it then known to *them?*" As long as there is a reasonable chance that you can do some good, you have an obligation to do everything in your power (see readings).

We also see another thing in this Talmudic lesson. The Gemorah tells us that God Himself had testified that one group was "perfectly righteous" (*Tzadikim Gemurim*), and that the other was "absolutely wicked" (*Resha'im Gemurim*). Can we imagine a man more perfect than one of whom God Himself testifies that he is "perfectly righteous," or one more wicked than he whom God calls "absolutely wicked?" Yet, from the context, we clearly see that even the most "perfectly righteous" have an obligation to improve even the most "absolutely wicked." No matter how perfect a person may be, he is not absolved from his responsibility toward his brethren, no matter how far they have strayed. The only exception is where it is absolutely certain that one can do no good, as discussed earlier.

We live in a time when literally millions of our fellow Jews are falling by the wayside. We only have to open our eyes and see the Torah being trampled in every corner. If we remain silent, we too will lose.

NOTES

1. Davar Belto, chapter 18.

READINGS

BIBLE

At the end of seven days, God's word came to me, saying:

Son of man, I have appointed you as a sentry to the house of Israel. When you hear a word from Me, warn them in My name.

When I say to a wicked man, "You must die," and you do not warn him—if you do not speak up to warn the wicked man of his evil ways so that he may live—then that wicked man shall die with his sin, but I will seek his blood from your hand.

But if you warn the wicked man, and he does not turn back from his wickedness—from his wicked way—then he shall die with his sins, but you will have saved his own soul.

And when a righteous man turns away from his righteousness and does wrong, I will place a stumbling block before him—he shall die. He shall die because you did not warn him of his sin— his righteousness shall not be remembered—but I will seek his blood from your hand.

But if you warn the righteous man not to sin, he will live because he has been warned, and you will have saved your own soul.

Ezekiel 3:16–21

God's word came to me, saying:

Son of man, speak to the children of your people, and say to them:

When I bring the sword upon a land, the people take one of their number and appoint him as a sentry. His task is to see when the sword comes upon the land, and sound the horn to warn the people.

If a person hears the horn, and does not heed the warning, then if the sword comes and takes him, his blood shall be upon his own head. He heard the sound of the horn and did not heed its warning—his blood shall be upon him—for if he had heeded the warning, he would have saved his own life.

But if the sentry sees the sword coming, and does not sound the horn, then the people are not warned. If the sword then comes and takes a soul among them, he will have died for his sin, but I will seek his blood from the sentry's hand.

You, son of man, I have appointed you as a sentry for the house of Israel. When you hear a word from Me, warn them in My name.

When I say to a wicked man, "You must die," and you do not warn him—if you do not speak up to warn the wicked man of his evil ways so that he may live—then that wicked man shall die with his sin, but I will seek his blood from your hand.

But if you warn the wicked man, and he does not turn back from his wicked ways—then he shall die with his sin, but you will have saved your own soul.

Ezekiel 33:1–9

———◆———

TALMUD

Anyone who has the opportunity to protest (the wrongdoings) of the members of his family and does not do so, is caught up in the sins of the members of his family.

(If one can do so) for the people of his city, he is caught up (in the sins) of the people of his city.

(If one can do so) for all the world, he is caught up (in the sins) of all the world.

Rav Pappa said, "The Jewish leadership (*Resh Galusa*) is there-fore caught up in the (sins of the) entire world."

This is very much like what Rabbi Chanina said. It is written (*Isaiah 3:14*), "God will enter into judgement with the elders of His people, and with their princes." If the princes sinned, how then did the elders sin? But this is because the elders did not protest the misdeeds of the princes . . . .

Rabbi Zeira said to Rabbi Simon, "Why do you not (speak up and) correct the Jewish leadership *(Resh Galusa)?*" He replied, "They will not pay any attention to me."

(Rabbi Zeira) said, "Even if they do not pay any attention, you should still (attempt) to correct them (according to the teaching of Rav Acha, son of Chanina)."

Rav Acha, son of Rav Chanina said: "Never did a good word leave God's mouth and then become transformed into evil, except in this case. It is written *(Ezekiel 9:4),* "God said (to the angel), go through the city—through Jerusalem—and make a mark on the foreheads of the people who sigh and cry for all the abominations that have been done there."

God said to Gabriel, "Go and make a mark with ink on the foreheads of the righteous, so that the angels of destruction should not attack them. Make a mark with blood on the foreheads of the wicked, so that they should be attacked by the angels of destruction."

The Attribute of Justice said before God, "Master of the Universe: How is one group different than the other?"

(God) replied, "One consists of the perfectly righteous, while the other consists of the absolutely wicked."

(The Attribute of Justice) said, "Master of the Universe, they were able to protest and did not do so."

(God) said, "It is revealed and known to Me that even if they would have protested, it would have had no effect."

(The Attribute) replied, "If it is revealed to You, was it then revealed to them?"

It is thus written *(Ibid. 9:6),* "Slay utterly, the old people, boys and girls, women and children, but do not touch anyone who has the mark on him—begin with My sanctuary." (Originally the order was not to touch anyone bearing the mark, but this was immediately changed, and the order was given to "begin with My sanctuary" *(Rashi).*) It is furthermore written, "They began with the elders who were in front of the Temple."

Rav Yosef taught: Do not read "My sanctuary" *(mikdashai),* but "My sanctified ones" *(MeKudeshai).* These are the people who kept the entire Torah, from A to Z. (Even these people perished because they did not correct the wicked.)

Shabbos 54b, 55a

When a prophet predicts good and it does not come true, then we can be certain that he is a false prophet. Any good thing that God decrees is never retracted, even if it is only stated conditionally.

There was actually only one instance where God reversed a good prediction. Before the destruction of the First Temple (*Bais HaMikdash*), God had promised that the righteous would not be killed together with the wicked. In this one case, God retracted His word (and the righteous were also destroyed). This is explained in detail (in the Talmud) in the tractate of *Shabbos*.

Rambam: Yad, Yesodey HaTorah 10:4

Rav Amram, son of Rav Shimon bar Abba, said in the name of Rab Shimon bar Abbah, who said this in the name of Rabbi Chanina: Jerusalem was only destroyed because people did not correct each other. It is written (*Lamentations 1:6*), "Her princes have become like rams." Just as one ram places its head near the tail of another, so the Jews of that generation hid their heads in the sand, and did nothing to correct one another.

Shabbos 119b

Abaya said: When a rabbi is well liked in a city, it does not mean that he is doing a good job. It is merely because he does not correct them with regard to heavenly affairs.

Kesubos 105b

Upon the heels of the Messiah (in the evil period before the Messiah comes) . . . people will not correct one another.

Sotah 49b

It is written (*Zephaniah 2:1*), "Correct yourself, and correct others." Resh Lakish said, "First correct yourself, and then correct others."

Baba Metzia 107b

Rabbi Shmuel bar Nachmani said in the name of Rabbi Yochanan: One who corrects others for the sake of heaven becomes worthy of God's portion. It is thus written (*Proverbs 28:23*), "He who corrects a person *after Me.* . . ." Besides that, a thread of grace will also be drawn over him, as it is written (*ibid.*), "He will find grace."

Tamid 28a

◆

MIDRASH

One who does not correct another is caught up in his sin. We have thus learned that one who has the opportunity to protest . . . and does not do so, is caught up in that sin.

. . .We have been taught that even the perfectly righteous are blamed for (the sins of) their generation (if they do not do anything about it). It is thus written (*Ezekiel 21:8*), "I will cut off from among you, the righteous and the wicked"—the righteous because they did not protest the (misdeeds of the) wicked.

Tanchuma, Mishpatim 7

Whoever knows how to correct others and does so brings pleasure to his Creator. It is thus written (*Proverbs 24:25*), "Those who correct others give Him pleasure, and a good blessing shall come upon them."

Tana DeBei Eliahu Rabbah 3

———◆———

RABBI ELIEZER OF MAINZ: SEFER YEREYIM

(Rabbi Eliezer was a disciple of Rabenu Tam, a leading Talmudical commentator)

When a person sees his friend doing something wrong and does not correct him, God holds him accountable. It is thus written *(Ezekiel 3:18)*, "If you do not warn him, then that wicked man shall die with his sin, but I will seek his blood from your hand."

We find that even the perfectly righteous are punished for this. The Gemorah says *(Shabbos 55a)*, "Begin with My sanctified ones—those who kept the Torah from A to Z." Even they were punished because they did not protest the actions of the wicked.

If you are certain that they will not accept your words, and they do not realize that they are doing wrong, then it is best to remain still. The Gemorah says *(Betza 30a)*, "Leave Israel alone— it is better that they sin unknowingly, and not sin knowingly."

. . .This, however, is only true when they are not aware that they are doing wrong. When they are aware of their wrongdoing, you must warn them, even though this will increase their guilt. . . . You must then correct them, even if they will not accept it. Regarding this, it is written *(Ezekiel 3:18)*, "He will die with his sin *(Avon)*, but I will seek his blood from your hand." The word *(Avon)* used here refers to purposeful sins. The Gemorah thus says *(Yoma 36b)*, "*Avon-os* are purposeful sins."

This might appear to contradict another Gemorah, which says *(Shabbos 55a)*: If the princes sinned, then how did the elders sin? God said, "Because they did not protest the wrongdoing of the princes." The Attribute of Justice asked, "Is it then not revealed before You that if they would have protested, the princes would not have accepted it?" God replied, "If it is revealed to Me, was it then revealed to them?"

[Note that the *Sefer Yereyim* uses a somewhat different reading of the Gemorah than that which exists in our editions.]

From this it would appear that if it was "revealed to them," they would no longer be obligated, even though the others were sinning purposefully.

What this teaches us, however, is that they are exempt from *punishment*. The Gemorah thus says *(Shavuos 39a)*, "A man shall stumble over his brother—over the sin of his brother," and the Gemorah says that this is speaking of a case where one had the opportunity to protest and did not do so. Nevertheless, one is not exempt from the commandment, "You must correct your neighbor," until he displays anger.

When you correct somebody, you must do so politely and gently. The Gemorah thus says *(Shabbos 34a)*, (that a man must ask his family), "Have you tithed, have you made the Eruv, have you kindled the Sabbath light?" Rabba bar bar Chanah comments, "One must say it gently, in order that they accept his words."

Sefer Yereyim 223, partially quoted in Sefer Mitzvos Gadol
(Smag), Positive Commandment No. 11

V

The Balance of Merit

How is a Jew who lives by the Torah to look at the Jewish world around him? What attitude should he have about those who ignore the teachings of the Torah completely, and live a life totally oblivious to Judaism?

As we have seen, we cannot simply ignore them. We must remain very much aware that we have a responsibility toward every Jew. In many cases, it will be certain that we cannot do any good, and we will therefore have to remain quiet. But there are countless Jews especially among our youth who still have an open mind, and it is toward these that we have a particular responsibility. We must do everything in our power to strengthen Judaism, and to create an atmosphere where all Jews will once again recognize their obligation to the Torah.

Most nonreligious Jews today have not abandoned the Torah out of spite or rebellion. Rather, they have done so out of ignorance, bcause they have never had the opportunity to really experience authentic Judaism. As we shall see, this gives them a very special status.

The Rambam (Maimonides) speaks of a similar situation with respect to the Karaites (see readings). As we know, the Karaites were a Jewish sect who believed only in the written Bible (*Kara*), but did not accept the oral tradition which is the basis of the Talmud and all Jewish Law. The Rambam unequivocally states that because of their lack of belief in the entire Torah, these Karaites are hardly to be considered Jews, and indeed, in a decision elsewhere, he states that they cannot even be counted toward a Minyan.[1] But when he speaks of their children who have never had the opportunity to experience authentic Judaism, he declares that they must be considered Jews in the fullest sense, and that they have the status of "an infant who was kidnapped by gentiles."[2]

The Gemorah speaks of an "infant kidnapped among gentiles," and states that even after he grows up, he has no responsibility above that of an unknowing sinner.[3] God does not hold a person responsible for something that is absolutely impossible to avoid. Therefore, if a person was kidnapped by gentiles as an infant, and raised without any knowledge of Judaism, he cannot be held responsible for not keeping the Torah. According to the Rambam, the same is true of one who is raised in a totally irreligious environment and was never able to experience a true Jewish life.

But what if such a person hears about Judaism later in life? In today's society, it is virtually impossible for a person never to hear about authentic Judaism, no matter how remote his background. What if such a person hears about the teachings of the Torah and sees religious Jews, and still does not accept authentic Judaism? Is he then considered responsible?

The Rambam writes that he is not. Since he was raised in a misguided manner, he is still considered to be acting against his will. Even when such a person sees authentic Judaism, he has no way of identifying with it, and he is therefore not responsible if he does not accept it.

It may be that the Rambam bases his teaching on another important rule. The Gemorah speaks of a case where a person is forced to sin, and then, as a result of this initial coercion, is eventually led to sin willingly.[4] The decision there is that since this person was initially brought into the sin against his will, he cannot later be held responsible for it. This is true even though he is eventually led to sin willingly.

The same is true in our case. A person who is raised from childhood not knowing the true meaning of Judaism cannot be held responsible if he fails to follow the Torah later. At worst, his lack of observance must be considered an "unwilling transgression." Even if he later learns about Judaism, he cannot be held responsible, since he has no way of identifying with it.

Indeed, this may be what the Gemorah means when it says that in the case of the ignorant, "even known transgressions are considered as if they were done out of ignorance."[5] If a person is raised in ignorance, even if he later finds out that he is doing wrong, he cannot be held fully responsible. The Gemorah thus ends by saying that even such ignorant people have "hope and a portion in God's delight."

There is also another important point that must be kept in mind. Because of the tremendous psychological and social obstacles that such a person must overcome to live according to the Torah, he is given a tremendous amount of merit when he actually succeeds in doing so. As our sages teach us, the level which can be achieved by a person who returns to Judaism of his own accord, can never be achieved by one who was born into a religious environment.[6] "According to suffering is reward,"[7] is an important maxim of Torah thought, and one who must overcome many barriers in order to embrace true Judaism is rewarded by God for every difficult step that he takes.

But how are we to approach those who have never really been exposed to true Judaism? What are we to say to these "kidnapped infants?" Here again, the Rambam gives us advice, and indeed, he may actually be expressing an opinion in Jewish law. He says that "it is fitting that we bring them back, and draw them with words of peace, until they return to the strength of the Torah."

First of all, the Rambam tells us that we have a responsibility to "bring them back." He also tells us how we must go about it— that we must "draw them with words of peace." We are not to argue with those who have never experienced Judaism, nor are we to engage in lengthy debates. Deep theological arguments never seem to prove very much, and they accomplish even less. What we must do is speak pleasantly with them, befriend them, and thus "draw them with words of peace."

Here again, the Rambam may be taking his cue from Hillel, who, as discussed earlier, taught that we should be like Aaron and, "love people, and bring them close to the Torah." Our sages derive this from a verse, which, according to tradition, speaks of Aaron.[8] It is written (*Malachi 2:6*), "He walked with Me in peace and uprightness, and turned many away from transgression." From this verse, we clearly see that the manner in which Aaron "turned many away from transgression" was by walking "in peace and uprightness."

This is by no means an easy task. We must be firm, and convince all Jews that the Torah way is the only true way of life for a Jew. Yet, at the same time, we must do so with "words of peace," being friendly rather than argumentative, persuasive, but not offensive. If we learn our lesson well, there is no limit to what we can accomplish. With God's help, we can once again bring all of our Jewish brethren "back to the strength of the Torah."

NOTES

1. *Tshuvos HaRambam (P'ear HaDor)* 71.
2. *Yad, Mamrim* 3:3. This is an accepted opinion, as we find in *Bais Yosef, Darkey Moshe* (2), on *Tur, Yoreh Deah* 159; *Shulchan Aruch, Yoreh Deah* 159:6 in *Hagah*.
3. *Shabbos* 68a, b, *Shavuos* 5a, *Yerushalmi Shabbos* 7:1 (40a). See *Yad, Shegagos* 2:6, 7:2.
4. *Kesubos* 41b, *Yerushalmi Sotah* 4:4 (20a), *BaMidbar Rabbah* 9:10, *Yad, Issurey Biah* 1:9. See *Magen Avraham* 204:20, *Biur HaGra ibid.* "*Im Ansuhu.*"
5. *Baba Metzia* 33b.
6. *Berachos* 34b, *Sanhedrin* 99a. Cf. *Koheles Rabbah* 1:27, *Tanna DeBei Eliahu Rabbah* 3, *Yalkut* 1:20, *Zohar* 1:39a, 2:106a, 2:113b, 3:16b, 3:202b; *Yad, Tshuvah* 7:4, *Chovos HaLevavos* 7:8, *Sefer Ha Yashar* 10, quoted in *HaGra, Orech Chaim* 53:8 "*Mi*", *Sefer Chasidim* 60, *Menoras HaMaor* 5:1:1:2 (277), 5:end (312), *Nesivos Olam, Nesiv Ha Tshuvah* 4. Also see Rashi, *Succah* 53a "*Elu*", *Pri Megadim, Eshel Avraham* 118:1.
7. *Avos* 5:23. Cf. Maharsha, *Berachos* 34b.
8. *Avos DeRabbi Nathan* 12:3. Cf. *Sanhedrin* 6b.

READINGS

———◆———

TALMUD

To say (to God), "The good shall bless you," is the way of atheism.

Megillah 4:9 (25a)

This is because one does not include the wicked in God's praise. Our sages (*Kerisos* 6b) taught that the *Chelbonah* (galbanum) was counted among the incenses (offered to God) even though it had a bad odor. God desires all to be in a single group.

Rashi on the above

A number of irreligious Jews lived in Rabbi Meir's neighborhood and they used to bother him very much. So annoyed was he that Rabbi Meir wanted to pray that they should die.

Beruria, his wife, said to him: "Why do you wish to do this? Is it because it is written (*Psalms 104:35*), "*Chata'im* shall cease to exist?" Who says that the word there is *Chot'im,* meaning sinners? The word used in the scripture is *Chata'im,* meaning sins. Furthermore, look at the end of this verse, "And the wicked shall be no more." Once sins (*Chata'im*) cease to exist, then "the wicked shall be no more." (Rather than pray for them to die,) you should pray that they return (to Judaism)."

Rabbi Meir prayed for them, and they eventually did return (to Judaism).

Berachos 10a

Resh Lakish said: It is written (*Song of Songs 6:7*), "Like a sliced pomegranate are Your empty ones." Even Your "empty ones" are filled with Mitzvos, like (seeds in) a pomegranate.

Rabbi Zeira said: It is written, (Genesis 27:27), "And (Isaac) smelled the perfume of (Jacob's) garments." Do not read "garments" (Begadd-av), but rebellion" (Boged-av). (Even in rebellion he smelled sweetly.)

Some irreligious Jews lived in the neighborhood of Rabbi Zeira. He used to associate with them, in order to bring them back (to the Torah). The other rabbis, however, did not consider this proper.

When (Rabbi Zeira) died, these (irreligious Jews) said, "This short man with burned legs (for Rabbi Zeira was short and had burned his legs in an accident) used to pray that God would have mercy on us. But now (that he is dead) who will pray for us?"

They thought about this, and eventually returned (to the Torah).

Sanhedrin 37a

———◆———

RAMBAM (MAIMONIDES)

A person who openly denies the authenticity of the Oral Torah is in the same category as all other heretics, people who deny that the Torah came from heaven, informers, and renegades. All of these are not counted as Jews.

This is only true, however, when an individual denies the Oral Torah on the basis of his own thoughts and opinions. Such a person follows his own limited intellect, and on his own, stubbornly denies the Oral Torah. He thus follows the footsteps of Tzaduk (the founder of the Saducees or *Tzadukim*), Baithus, and their followers.

This, however, is not true of the children and descendants of those who have gone astray. These individuals are raised among the Karaites and have been convinced by their parents. They are therefore in the same category as a person kidnapped by gentiles as an infant and raised by them. He may not be eager to observe the commandments, but he is considered to be unwillingly negligent.

Even though such a person may later find out that he is a Jew and see other Jews practicing their religion, he is still considered to be unwillingly negligent, since he was raised in such a misguided manner.

The same is true of those who follows the ways of their fathers who are heterodox Karaites.

It is therefore fitting to bring them back, and draw them with words of peace, until they return to the strength of the Torah.

Yad, Mamrim 3:3

One should not repel those who do not keep the Sabbath, nor should one despise them. Rather, one must draw them close, encouraging them to keep the commandments.

Our sages teach us that even if a person transgresses willingly, we must accept him when he comes to synagogue to pray, and not shame him in any manner. They derive this from King Solomon's words *(Proverbs 6:30)*, "Do not despise a thief if he steals to satisfy his soul when it hungers." They interpret this to mean that one should not despise irreligious Jews when they come covertly to steal Mitzvos.

Maamar Kidush HaShem, end

———◆———

RABBI BACHYA IBN PAKUDA: CHOVOS HA-LEVAVOS

Some people (express their love for God) by teaching others to serve God.

. . . A person can reach the highest level in rectifying his own soul before God, and he can attain the heights of the angels with respect to good traits, proper habits, effort in serving his Creator, and purity of love. Still, such a person's merit is not as great as that of one who teaches others how to return to the right path and leads the wicked back to serve God. Such a person's merit is multiplied according to theirs, every minute of every day.

We can understand this with an example. Two businessmen come to a new territory. One of them makes a tenfold profit on his merchandise, but he only has one thing to sell. He therefore earns a hundred dollars.

The other merchant only makes a twofold profit on his merchandise. He has much to sell, however, and therefore earns ten thousand dollars.

Even though the first merchant made a tenfold profit on his merchandise, his entire profit was only 90 dollars. . . . The second merchant, on the other hand, made a profit of 5,000 dollars, even though he only made a twofold profit on his goods.

The same is true in our case. If a person only rectifies his own soul, his merit is correspondingly much less. One who rectifies both his own soul and the souls of others, on the other hand, multiplies his merit according to the merit of everyone whom he rectifies before God.

Our sages thus teach us (*Avos 5:18*), "if a person makes others worthy, sin will not come to his hand." They likewise taught (*Ibid.*), "Moses himself was worthy, and he also made many others worthy. Therefore, the merit of the multitude was counted toward him. It is thus written (*Deuteronomy 33:21*), 'He did God's righteousness, his judgement was with Israel.' "

It is written (*Proverbs 24:25*), "He who corrects others will find delight, and a good blessing shall come upon him." We likewise find (*Malachi 2:6*), "The true Torah was in his mouth . . . (he walked with Me in peace and uprightness, and turned many from transgressions)." It is furthermore written (Daniel 12:3), "(The wise shall shine like the brightness of the sky) and those who turn multitudes to righteousness, like the stars, forever and ever."

The Creator therefore commanded us to correct the irreligious, as it is written (*Leviticus 19:17*), "You must correct your neighbor." . . . It is furthermore written (*Proverbs 28:23*), "He who corrects a person follows Me, he shall find grace."

Chovos HaLevavos, Shaar Ahavas HaShem 6

———◆———

RABBI YOSEF BABAD: MINCHAS CHINUCH

Besides the commandment, "You must correct your neighbor" (bringing others back to the right path) also involves the commandment (*Leviticus 19:16*) "You shall not stand idly by the blood of your neighbor." This commandment obligates us to save a person who is, for example, drowning. (Bringing him back to the Torah) is not less significant.

Also involved is the commandment (*Deuteronomy 22:2*), "You must return a person's loss to him." As our sages teach us (*Baba Kama 81b*), this commandment also obligates us to restore a person's life and health. Therefore, if you can save a person from sin, which involves a loss of both body and soul, you certainly have the responsibility to save him and bring him back to the right path.

If a person spitefully eats non-kosher food, blatantly violates the Sabbath, or embraces another religion, then (our sages teach us that) he is no longer considered "your brother" with respect to returning a lost article and similar cases (*Avodah Zara 26b*). It is therefore possible that you do not have an obligation to correct such a person, since he is no longer considered "your neighbor."

Nevertheless, in my opinion, if there is any question whatsoever that he might accept your words, then you have the obligation to correct him. You must bring him back to the path of righteousness, so that he will once again be counted as "your brother." (See *Avodah Zara, loc. cit.*)

Minchas Chinuch 139:4

———◆———

RABBI NACHMAN OF BRESLOV

Our sages teach us (*Avos 1:6*), "Judge every person on the balance of merit."

Even if a person is absolutely wicked, you must search in order to find some good in him. Small as it might be, as far as that good is concerned, even such a person is not wicked, and therefore, when you find this good you are placing him on the "balance of merit." In this manner, you can actually bring such a person to the "balance of merit" and draw him back to God.

It is thus written (*Psalm 37:10*), "A little more, and there will be no wicked, and if you look well at his place, he is no longer there."

This verse is also teaching us that we must presume each person's merit. Even though a person may seem absolutely wicked, you must still hunt and search to find some small good, where he is not evil. The verse therefore says, "A little more, and there will be no wicked." You must seek in him "a little more" good (than is apparent), for with respect to this good, he is not wicked.

Let us assume that this person is actually wicked. Still, is it at all possible that he has absolutely no redeeming merit? Is it at all possible that he has never done any good in his entire lifetime? Consider this, and you discover that you must find "a little more" good in him. With respect to this good, he is not wicked, and therefore, when you find it, you are judging him "on the balance of merit."

When you do this, however, you are literally lifting that person up from the "balance of liability" to the "balance of merit." In doing this, you can actually bring him back (to God).

This is the meaning of the verse, "A little more, and there will be no wicked." No person is actually wicked with respect to that "little more" good that you can find in him.

Then, "If you look well at his place, he is no longer there." If you look well enough, and observe that person's place and situa-tion, then "he is no longer there" in that place. For if you look well enough to find some speck of virtue—that "little more" good—and judge him on the balance of merit, then you actually convey him (to another place)—from the "balance of guilt" to the "balance of merit." Then indeed, "if you look well at his place, he is no longer there."

Likutey Moharan 282

VI

A Time for Action

*O*ur sages teach us *(Baba Metzia 107b)*, "First correct your-self, and then correct others." It is indeed a great Mitzvah to bring others close to the Torah. First, however, one must strengthen his own commitment to Torah.

Yeshiva years are a time when one must concentrate on self-improvement. During one's youth, one must make the study of Torah his full-time occupation, striving for greatness in Torah. A

This chapter is based on a call to action issued by HaGaon Rabbi Moshe Feinstein to Yeshiva students, in view of the extraordinary nature of our times. We believe that it has broad implications with respect to every individual's responsibility to act on behalf of his fellow Jew.

The talk upon which this chapter is based was originally delivered at a meeting sponsored by the P'eylim at the Agudas Israel of Boro Park on 22 Adar, 5733. The talk was transcribed by this author, and was originally published in June, 1973 issue of the *Jewish Observer*.

student must use every emotion to bring himself close to Torah. Even traits which are generally considered negative, such as envy, must be harnessed to further a person's growth in Torah. The Gemorah thus advises (*Baba Basra 21a*), "Envy among scribes increases wisdom." Like King David, the cry of the Yeshiva student must be (*Psalm 63:2*), "My soul thirsts for You," and this must supersede all other involvements. Only after one has developed his own powers in Torah can he assume responsibility for others.

This sequence is reflected in our prayers, when we ask God to give us the power to "learn and to teach." First we must learn, then we can teach others.

Today, however, a crisis situation exists, and it is most acute. While there were times when we could keep ourselves distant from the forces of darkness, they are now closing in, even threatening the most sheltered communities of those loyal to the Torah. In addition, many estranged Jews are now searching for the truth of the Torah. These are exceptional times. We must therefore examine our accepted priorities in order to determine who is to be charged with the responsibility of battling to better our situation, and under what conditions.

The first step in this examination is the establishment of guidelines. Rules must be strictly adhered to, even when bringing people close to the Torah. Unless one follows these rules, he can do more damage than good.

The most basic rule is that we must follow the directives of our current Torah leadership. This is especially true in the area of reaching out to those who have been estranged from the Torah, where there is always a temptation to rationalize, compromise and make concessions. While every discipline has its experts, and people generally recognize that one can succeed only if he follows their advice, in the field of reaching out to the uncommitted there are too many self-styled experts, who believe that they know more than our leading Torah authorities. Too often, their ideas can accomplish more harm than good. Worse yet, they consider such matters outside the realm of our Torah leaders' expertise, and feel that they are not obligated to follow their teachings, even making light of their advice. This approach in itself is as great an evil as that which they are trying to overcome. It does violence to a central aspect of the Jewish commitment, namely that the authority vested in the Torah leadership of each generation is an integral part of the Oral Torah (*Torah SheBaal Peh*).

The Gemorah tells of a heathen who came to Hillel and asked to be converted to Judaism (*Shabbos 31a*). As Rashi explains, this heathen was willing to accept both the Written Torah and the Oral Torah—but he refused to recognize the interpretations of Shammai and Hillel as part of the Oral Torah spoken by God. Nonetheless, Hillel accepted him. As Rashi continues, Hillel was confident that once he had taught the heathen, the latter would come to depend on him. Rashi's explanation of the incident illustrates the belief that the Oral Torah is totally dependent upon the teachings of the Torah leaders of each generation (*Gedoley HaDor*).

This authority must be granted to the leaders of each genera-tion, regardless of their merit with respect to the leaders of previous generations. Our sages thus teach us (*Rosh HaShanah 25b*), "Jephthah in his generation was like Samuel in his." Even though the prophet Samuel was undoubtedly greater than Jephthah, the latter still merited ultimate respect as the Torah leader of his own generation. Greater sages may have lived in earlier times, but our obligation is to follow those of our own age.

A person who does not accept the Torah leaders of his genera-tion cannot claim to believe in the Oral Torah. Therefore, a person who fails to follow our Torah leaders, even if he is religious in every other respect, is not qualified to lead others in reaching out to the uncommitted.

When presented with the opportunity to engage in endeavors outside of his own personal growth, the Yeshiva student will normally defer to others. He assumes that there are others who are equally qualified to handle the problems at hand, if not more so. Now that so many nonreligious individuals are seeking the truth, we might hope that there would be enough interested people who are qualified to meet their needs. Unfortunately, this is not so. The very ones who claim to offer them truth are often further from it than the seekers—and might even be described as being ensnared in a form of conceptual idolatry.

The Torah warns us (*Leviticus 19:4*), "Do not turn to the idols." The Gemorah (*Shabbos 149a*) explains that this also refers to conceptual idols, which are ideologies not based on the Torah. Unless a person follows the Torah meticulously, he can even make idols out of his own ideas. This unstructured and uninhibited "freedom of thought" is frequently the hallmark of many who are engaged in enlightening those who are seeking, and it unquestionably disqualifies them from the task.

Yet, those who seek guidance must be led by somebody. He who leads others must be extremely firm in his faith. He must not follow his own whims, but must base his entire ideology on God's Torah. He must also be meticulous in adhering to the teachings of our Torah leaders.

This leaves us none but the *Ben Torah,* whose spiritual stamina is fortified by the Torah as taught by the leaders of our great Yeshivos. Only he is equipped to address the masses and lead them back to the truth.

The Yeshiva student may insist that he can offer the world much more by devoting himself fully to his Torah studies, which is his prime obligation. A person is not permitted to interrupt Torah study for any Mitzvah, unless it is a personal obligation (such as putting on Tefillin, or reciting the Sh'ma). Indeed, Moses, who was our people's greatest teacher and prime redeemer, would have actually preferred to abstain from leading the Jewish people. He realized that he could accomplish much more through his personal involvement in the Torah.

Thus, when God wanted to send Moses to lead the Jewish people, the latter responded (*Exodus 4:13*), "Send whomever (else) you would send." The Midrash (*VaYikra Rabbah 1:5*) teaches us that Moses did not want to assume this leadership, and only did so because there was no one else who could. It states:

> God said to Moses (*Exodus 3:10*), "Now go, and I will send you to Pharaoh."
> Rabbi Elazar said, ". . .This teaches us that (God said), 'If you do not redeem them, then there is no one else who can.' "
> At the Red Sea, Moses again stood to the side. God then told him (*Exodus 14:16*), "Lift up your rod . . . and split it."

This teaches us that (God had said), "If you do not split the sea, then no one else can."

At Sinai, Moses again stood to the side. God told him (*Exodus 24:12*), "Come up to Me to the mountain." Here again, God had said, "If you do not come, then no one else can."

Finally, when the Tabernacle (*Ohel Moed*) was erected, Moses again stood to the side. God told him, "How long will you continue to lower yourself? At this time, you are the only one."

We know that this is true, because the Lord never called to any man other than Moses. The Torah thus says (*Leviticus 1:1*), "And He called to Moses."

The Midrash here speaks of the four main tasks that Moses had to accomplish. In each case, we find that Moses did not want to undertake the task, and did not do so until commanded directly by God.

The Yeshiva student's predilection to abstain therefore has a precedent. By the same token, however, so does the need for him to become actively involved in special circumstances have a similar precedent. Just as Moses responded to the voice of authority when it told him, "You must, because there is no one else," so too must our Yeshiva students. As mentioned earlier, there are no others who are qualified for the task. Under such circumstances, even Torah study must be interrupted.

Another factor that increases the obligation of those who are capable of bringing others close to the Torah is the fact that many people who are far from Torah life can be categorized as a *Tinok SheNishba*—a person held captive by gentiles since infancy (*Yoreh Deah 159:6*). It is a Mitzvah—an obligation—to bring such individuals back to the Torah and Judaism (*Yad, Mamrim 3:3*). When there is no one else to accomplish this, then a person must even take time from his Torah studies to do so.

In summary, one must emulate Moses, who was a leader because he had no choice.

There is always the defense against active involvement in teaching others: Must I sacrifice my own growth?

The Gemorah teaches us (*Kidushin 29b, Yoreh Deah 245:2*), "A man and his son must both study Torah: When it is possible for only one of them to do so, a man's personal needs take precedence over those of his son." A person may not even take time from his own Torah studies to teach his son, unless he knows that his son's potential is greater than his own. This is a highly significant point. If a person's own studies take precedence over teaching his own child, then they certainly take precedence over teaching strangers.

On the basis of this, another teaching may appear somewhat difficult to understand. The Gemorah (*Eruvin 54b*) tells us that Rabbi Preda had a student with whom he reviewed each lesson 400 times. As a reward for this, 400 extra years were allotted to his life, and everyone in his generation was guaranteed a place in the World to Come.

One would assume that Rabbi Preda could have gained more knowledge had he used this time for his own study. To be sure, when one teaches, he also learns, as Rabbi Chanina stated (*Taanis 7a*), "Much have I learned from my teachers, more from my companions, and most of all from my students." Rabbi Chanina's maxim, however, obviously did not apply to a student such as Rabbi Preda's. In addition, no one can grow exclusively from teaching, and therefore, each individual must also study for himself.

One important lesson is apparent from this. Even though an individual's own studies take precedence over another's, he must still find time to teach others.

A major question, however, remains: How much time can and must a person devote to this task?

A rule for the proportion of one's resources that he must give to others can be inferred from the laws of charity. (We find a similar parallel in *Tanna DeBei Eliahu Rabbah 27.*) A person must have enough to take care of his own personal needs before he gives to charity (*Tur Yoreh Deah 251*). Nevertheless, this is not to be taken so literally as to totally exempt a person who does not have everything he needs from giving charity (*Yoreh Deah 248:1*). There is always some measure that one must do for others.

The same is true of our own Torah needs. There is no question that a person's primary obligation is his own studies. One can never say that he has amassed enough to meet his personal needs, for the Torah is . . . longer than the earth, and broader than the sea" (Job 11:9). One must therefore give his own studies prece- dence, but this must not be absolute. A person must also act on behalf of others.

In the case of charity, one must give a tenth of his income to the poor (Yoreh Deah 249:1). Likewise, one must spend one tenth of his time working on behalf of others, bringing them close to the Torah. If a person is endowed with greater resources, he must correspondingly spend more of his time with others.

A person cannot even contemplate involvement with fellow Jews in more worldly circumstances—even for the higher purpose of winning them to a Torah commitment—without taking note of the risks and pitfalls that abound today. It is in place to issue words of caution, as well as words of encouragement, in this regard.

Today's situation has many special pitfalls particular to our times. Many people feel that they can partake of the worldly along with Torah. They do not realize that this world is the portion of Esau, and not that of Jacob (Devarim Rabbah 1:17). They want to indulge in all worldly delights in a kosher manner— should a commodity or activity carry a kosher label, they even consider it a Mizvah to pursue it. This brings people to lose valuable time from their Torah studies, and in some respects the situation has reached tragic proportions.

Most certainly then, if a person hopes to bring others to Torah, he must make Torah the primary focus of his life. It is thus incumbent upon ourselves to divorce ourselves from worldly pursuits to the greatest extent possible. The Gemorah (Yoma 69b) tells us that our sages once went so far as to contemplate destroy- ing all worldly desires completely. The only reason why they did not fully execute this plan was because some measure of worldly desire is essential for the continuance of the course of nature. Nevertheless, they sought to reduce the pursuit of worldly desires to the greatest degree possible.

When faced with this warning to avoid worldly entanglements and distractions, one might well be reluctant to engage in any pursuit other than Torah study—even for the ultimate purpose of bettering the lot of others through bringing the uncommitted to the Torah. But the current situation makes urgent demands on us. As King David said *(Psalm 119:126)*, "It is a time to work for God, they have abandoned Your Torah." One must indeed devote the major portion of his time to Torah study, but there are times when we must set Torah study aside and implement Torah action for God's sake, to bring the truth to others.

When a person does this in the manner prescribed by our Torah leadership, then God will give him strength so that association with people estranged from our Torah will not harm him.

When one follows the ways of Torah, he is indeed protected by God from all harm. It is in this spirit that the Torah tells us *(Genesis 33:18)*, "Jacob came complete to the city of Shechem." Rashi comments that he returned from Laban complete in body, possessions and Torah. He had followed the way of the Torah, and no harm could befall him.

VII

The Commandment in Jewish Law

◆ 1 ◆

If a person sees another Jew[1] sinning[2] or following the wrong path, he is required to correct him and attempt to set him right. We are thus commanded *(Leviticus 19:17)*, "You must correct your neighbor."[3] Even though this commandment specifically only refers to a person violating a Biblical commandment, we are required to correct any person who is doing wrong.[4]

◆ 2 ◆

Just as a person makes every attempt to save a friend from physical harm, so should he attempt to save him from spiritual harm.[5] We can learn this from God Himself, as it is written *(Proverbs 3:12)*, "For one who God loves, He corrects."[6] A person should desire for his friends the same spiritual benefits that he wishes for himself, and it is thus written (*Proverbs 5:16*), "Let your springs be dispersed abroad."[7]

◆ 3 ◆

A person should correct himself before he attempts to correct others.[8] Otherwise, they will not accept his correction.[9]

◆ 4 ◆

Just as we are required to correct others, so are we required to accept correction. The Torah thus states (*Deuteronomy 10:16*), "Therefore, cut away the thickening of your hearts, and stiffen your necks no more."[10]

◆ 5 ◆

It is therefore very important to accept correction, as the Scripture teaches us (*Proverbs 24:25*), "Correction brings delight, and a good blessing shall come upon them."[11] A person who accepts correction is considered wise, as we find (*Ibid. 9:8*), "Correct a wise man and he will love you."[12] On the other hand, one who refuses to accept correction is not likely to repent,[13] and will die with his sin, as it is written (*Ibid. 15:10*), "He who hates correction shall die."[14]

◆ 6 ◆

It is therefore the responsibility of every community to encourage its spiritual leaders to speak out and correct them.[15] A congregation that discourages its spiritual leaders from correcting them is considered a congregation of sinners. Regarding them it is written (*II Chronicles 36:16*), "They mocked the messengers of God and despised His words . . . until God's wrath arose against His people and there was no remedy."[16]

♦ 7 ♦

Just as one is required to correct others with regard to sins against God, so should he do so with respect to sins against his own person. Therefore, if a person is wronged, he should not keep the hurt to himself, but should speak out to the person who wronged him.[17] We can learn this lesson from Abraham, as we find (*Genesis 19:17*), "And Abraham admonished Abimelech."[18] It is forbidden to bear hatred because of such a wrong, as the Torah states (*Leviticus 19:17*), "You shall not hate your brother in your heart,[19] (but) you must correct your neighbor."[20]

♦ 8 ♦

It is therefore forbidden to carry a grudge and refuse to speak to the person who has committed this wrong.[21] We are thus taught that the one who refuses to speak to his neighbor for three days is considered his enemy[22] and is guilty of violating this commandment not to hate.[23]

♦ 9 ♦

It is similarly forbidden to attempt to cover up one's hurt while keeping it in his heart. It is thus written (*Psalm 28:3*), "Draw me not away with the wicked . . . who speak peace with their neighbors, but have evil in their hearts."[24] Nevertheless, if one wishes to forgive the wrongdoer in his heart and not say anything, it is commendable to do so.[25]

♦ 10 ♦

When first correcting a person, one should begin as politely and as gently as possible, speaking to him privately[27] so as not to shame him in any way.[28] If one knows that the person will be ashamed at the mention of the sin, he should not even correct him privately, but should merely hint at the sin and try to draw the person away from it.[29]

◆ 11 ◆

If the wrongdoer accepts correction immediately, no more is required, and he should be blessed.[30] If it is not accepted, however, one must correct him as many times as necessary in order to bring him to the right path.[31]

◆ 12 ◆

One is required to correct a wrongdoer as long as there is any chance that it might have a positive effect. However, if he shows signs of anger,[32] becomes insulting,[33] scornful,[34] or simply refuses to listen,[35] one must stop.[36] It is thus written (*Proverbs 9:8*), "Do not correct a scorner, lest he hate you."[37]

◆ 13 ◆

If a person does not accept correction privately, one should correct him in the presence of his friends.[38] If this still does not have any effect, one should correct him publicly,[39] shame him,[40] or do anything else in his power to bring him back to the right path.[41]

◆ 14 ◆

One is only required to begin correcting a person privately if he sins privately. If one is committing a sin in public, however, where others may learn from him, then he should be publicly corrected.[42]

◆ 15 ◆

Where only personal injury[43] is involved, one may only speak up privately, and under no condition shame the person who has committed this wrong. The Torah thus says *(Leviticus 19:17)*, "You must correct your neighbor, (but) do not bear a sin because of him." That is, you should not bear a sin by publicly shaming him.[44]

♦ 16 ♦

Although one is required to prevent another from sinning in any way possible, one is not required to expose himself to any harm in the process. Therefore, one is not required to correct another if he fears that the latter will take revenge and harm him.[45]

♦ 17 ♦

When a person must correct an entire congregation, he may speak out and need not be concerned lest he shame them.[46] However, one is only required to correct a correction where there is a chance that they might accept it.[47] If one is certain that his words will not be accepted, he is only required to correct them once, in order that they not be able to plead ignorance.[48] Beyond that, we are taught that just as one has an obligation to speak up when his words will be accepted, so must he refrain from speaking up when they will not.[49]

♦ 18 ♦

If one sees his father, rabbi, or teacher[50] violating any law,[51] he is required to correct him, just as he must correct any other person. Even though this might appear disrespectful, God's honor comes before that of any human being,[52] as we are taught *(Proverbs 21:30)*, "There is no wisdom, understanding or counsel against God."[53] Nevertheless, out of respect, one should do this as indirectly as possible, preferably posing it as a question, "Have you not taught us that this is wrong?"[54]

◆ 19 ◆

If a person sees his rabbi or teacher engaged in some questionable action, if Torah law is involved, he should question the action immediately. Where only rabbinical law is involved, however, he should not question it until after the fact.[55]

◆ 20 ◆

Even though it is normally forbidden to render any decision in the presence of one's teacher or rabbi, one may do so in order to prevent another person from sinning. Where God's name may be desecrated, we do not render honor, even to a rabbi.[56]

◆ 21 ◆

If a person is knowingly violating any law, one is required to correct him, even though he is certain that he will be ignored.[57] If he is certain that his words will be useless, however, then he is not punished for the other's sin if he neglects to correct him.[58]

◆ 22 ◆

Even if a person is doing something wrong unknowingly, and it is certain that he will ignore any correction, one is still required to correct him where any law expressedly written in the Torah is concerned.[59] When a law is written in the Torah, ignorance of the law is no excuse.[60]

◆ 23 ◆

If a law is not written in the Torah, however, then the oath regarding mutual responsibility does not apply to it.[61] Therefore, in such a case, if a person is doing wrong unknowingly, and it is certain that the correction will be ignored, then nothing need be said.[62] In such a case, we say that it is better for people to do wrong unknowingly, than to do so knowingly.[63]

◆ 24 ◆

Where people have become accustomed to do something publicly, it is assumed that they will not accept correction with regard to it.[64] However, if there is even a chance that they are doing wrong knowingly,[65] or that the correction will have a positive effect,[66] then one is required to speak up, even where only rabbinical law is concerned.[67]

◆ 25 ◆

We only say that it is better for people to sin unknowingly where very few minor transgressions are involved. However, where people are violating many laws unknowingly, we must correct them in every case,[68] lest our entire religion gradually be forgotten.[69]

◆ 26 ◆

Similarly, we only say that it is better for people to sin unknowingly where an old established custom[70] involving all the people is involved. Where only a few people are involved, however, they must be corrected, in order that others not learn from them.[71]

◆ 27 ◆

Although one is required to correct another even where it will be ignored, one is not required to correct a person who is completely nonreligious and nonbelieving. Similarly, one need not correct a person who habitually sins out of spite.[72] The Torah tells us (*Leviticus 17:19*), "You must correct your *neighbor*"—and such individuals are not considered "your neighbor."[73] Nevertheless, if

there is any chance whatsoever that one may have a good influence on them, one is required to make every effort.[74]

◆ 28 ◆

However, a person who has been brought up in a nonreligious
environment,[75] where he never had the opportunity to learn
about Judaism,[76] is like a child who was abducted by gentiles,[77]
and is not considered to be doing wrong purposely.[78] Even if he is
later exposed to authentic Judaism, he is not to be blamed for
rejecting it, since it is almost impossible to overcome one's childhood upbringing.[79] Therefore, such a person is not to be counted
among the nonbelievers,[80] and he should be approached with love
and with every attempt to bring him back to the teachings of our
faith.[81]

◆ 29 ◆

Just as one is required to correct a wrongdoer verbally, so is one
required[82] to physically stop or prevent a person from sinning
wherever possible.[83] However, if a person is sinning unknowingly[84] or only violating a rabbinical law,[85] he need not be
stopped where it would involve a public spectacle.[86] In such
cases, we say that preserving human dignity comes even before
preventing sin.[87] Nevertheless, if the sin is likely to be continued
for a long time afterwards, and this is the only opportunity, one is
required to act even in such cases.[88] In any event, where such
action is likely to violate the law of the land, no action need be
taken.[89]

◆ 30 ◆

One who has the ability to influence others and prevent them
from doing wrong is considered responsible for their sins if he fails
to do whatever he can. This is true whether one can only influence the members of his own family, or whether he can influence

the entire community.[90] Concerning this, God told His prophet (*Ezekiel 3:18*), "If you do not speak up to warn the wicked man from his evil way to save his life, then the wicked man shall die with his sin, but I will require his blood from your hand."[91] One who neglects to prevent others from sinning is also included in the Biblical malediction (*Deuteronomy 27:26*), "Cursed is the man who does not uphold all the words of this Torah."[92]

◆ 31 ◆

Nevertheless, as soon as a person corrects another according to the law, he is released from this responsibility.[93] The Scripture thus states (*Ezekiel 3:9*), "If you warn the wicked man to turn from his wicked way, and if he does not turn from it, then he shall die with his sin, but you will have saved your soul."[94] Even if the correction has no effect, one is still rewarded for the attempt.[95] It is written (*Proverbs 28:23*), "He who corrects a man shall in the end find more favor than he with the flattering tongue."[96]

◆ 32 ◆

One who in any way causes another to do some good, or assists him in doing it, shares the other's reward.[97] Therefore, for example, one can support another who is engaged in Torah study, in return for a share of his merit.[98] This is only true, however, before the good deed is completed. After the deed is done, all the money in the world cannot buy a share of its merit.[99]

◆ 33 ◆

Similarly, one who causes another to sin shares the responsibility for the sin.[100] If one causes another to sin unknowingly, he can often bear legal as well as moral responsibility for it.[101] It is written (*Proverbs 28:10*), "He who causes the upright to go astray on an evil way, shall himself fall into his own pit."[102]

◆ 34 ◆

Although one is required to make every effort to prevent another from sinning, one is not required to put out any money to do so.[103] Nevertheless, where one is bringing another back to Judaism completely, then he must make any expenditure necessary, since this comes under the heading of loving God with all one's possessions.[103] One is not required to jeopardize life or limb to prevent another from sinning.[104] However, where there is no actual probability of danger, one may not refrain from acting merely because of an unfounded fear or timidity.[105] The Torah thus commands us (*Deuteronomy 1:17*), "You shall not be afraid of any man."[106]

◆ 35 ◆

One is not allowed to sin in order to benefit another.[107] Therefore, one should not violate even a minor law in order to prevent another person from purposely committing a greater sin.[108]

◆ 36 ◆

However, where one may be responsible for the other person's sin,[109] or where one has a special responsibility toward the wrongdoer,[110] then one may violate a minor law[111] in order to prevent a serious sin.[112]

◆ 37 ◆

Similarly, if another person is being forced to sin, it is permitted to violate a lesser law in order to save him.[113] If the situation arose through that person's purposeful negligence, however, then he is considered a purposeful wrongdoer.[114]

◆ 38 ◆

Before violating any law for the sake of another, one must be very careful to gauge which is the more important. Thus, for example, violating the Sabbath is considered among the very worst sins, and therefore, one may not violate the Sabbath[116] in order to save another person[117] who is being forced to commit even the most serious[118] sin.[119] If something is only prohibited by rabbinical law on the Sabbath, however, the law may be violated in order to prevent another from transgressing any negative command-ment,[120] as long as he is not doing it purposefully.[121]

◆ 39 ◆

Although one may not violate the Sabbath in order to prevent an individual from sinning, one may do so to save an entire com-munity that is being forced to sin.[122]

◆ 40 ◆

If a person is being forced to leave the fold of Judaism completely, it is permitted to violate the Sabbath in any manner[123] in order to save him,[124] since it is better to violate one Sabbath, in order that he may keep many.[125] This is true even where it is not certain that he can be saved.[126]

◆ 41 ◆

Even where a community is not responsible for a very young child's religious training,[127] they must violate the Sabbath to save him from leaving the fold of Judaism,[128] since if he is taken away from Judaism as a child, he will remain away as an adult.[129] If a child's parents do not wish to violate the Sabbath to save their child, they can be forced to do so by the community.[130]

◆ 42 ◆

If a person wishes to leave the Jewish fold voluntarily, without coercion, then he is considered to be a purposeful sinner, and we may not violate the Sabbath to save him.[131] In such a case, however, it is permitted to violate any rabbinical law in order to save him.[132] Nevertheless, if he is likely to remain irreligious and cause others to sin, no attempt should be made to stop him even if this does not require the violation of any law on our part. It is thus written *(Hosea 4:17)*, "Ephraim is joined to idols, let him alone."[133]

May God bring all His people back to serve Him with a perfect heart, Amen.

NOTES

1. But not a non-Jew, cf. Rashi, *Sanhedrin* 75a *"Velm."*
2. Even in violation of a positive commandment, cf. *Sefer Chasidim* 5, *Makor Chesed ad loc.* 5:1; *Ginas Vardim, Orech Chaim* 3:15.
3. *Sifra, Yalkut* (1:613), *Zohar* (3:85b), *Ramban, ad loc., Archin* 16b, Rif. *Baba Metzia* 17a, *Yad, Deyos* 6:7, *Sefer HaMitzvos*, positive 205, *Sefer Mitzvos Gadol (Smag)*, positive 11, *Chinuch* 239, *Reshis Chochmah, Shaar HaAnavah* 5 (New York 5728) 227d. Also see *Mishpatei Sh'muel* (Vilna 1916) *"Shematsa DeTochacha"* pp. 40a–44a; *Mitzvas Tochacha* (Jerusalem 1951); *Orech Mesharim* 31.
4. *Berachos* 31b, *Tosefos ad loc. "Davar."*
5. *Mesilas Yesharim* 19 (28b). Cf. *Archin* 16b, *Berashis Rabbah* 54:3, *Yalkut* 1:95.
6. *Zohar* 3:85b, *Reshis Chochmah ibid.* 228a.
7. Rambam, *Perek HaHatzalah* p. 6.
8. *Baba Metzia* 107b, *Baba Basra* 60b, *Sanhedrin* 18a, 19a, *Yerushalmi Taanis* 2:1 (8b), Rashi, Radak on *Zephaniah* 2:1.
9. *Sefer Chasidim* 5. Cf. *Baba Basra* 15b, *Archin* 16b, Rashbam, *Baba Basra* 60b *"HisKosheshu."*
10. *Sefer Mitzvos Katan (Smak)* 9, quoted in *Cheredim* 1:32. Cf. Ramban *ad loc.*
11. *Tamid* 28a, Rashi *ad loc. "SheNe'mar."* Yalkut 2:961, *Reshis Chochmah loc. cit.* 228b, *Shnei Luchos HaBris, "Toldos Adam"* (Jerusalem 5720) 1:3a.
12. *Archin* 16b, Rif, *Baba Metzia* 17a, *Sefer Mitzvos Katan loc. cit.*
13. *Yad, Tshuvah* 4:2.

14. *Shaarey Tshuvah* (R. Yonah) 2:11. *Cf.* Ralbag *ad loc.*
15. *Yad, Tshuvah* 4:2, *Sefer Chasidim* 19. *Cf. Yalkut* 2:533.
17. *Archin* 16b. *Yad, Deyos* 6:6, *Sefer Mitzvos Gadol,* negative-5, *Kitzur Shul-chan Aruch* 29:15. *Cf. Tanna DeBei Eliahu Rabbah* 18 (91a).
18. Ramban on Leviticus 19:17. *Cf. Berashis Rabbah* 54:3, *Yalkut* 1:95.
19. *Pesachim* 113b, *Nedarim* 9:4 (62b), *Sotah* 3a, *Archin* 16b, *Yad, Deyos* 6:5, *Sefer HaMitzvos,* negative 302, *Sefer Mitzvos Gadol,* negative 5, *Chinuch* 238.
20. *Yad, Deyos* 6:6.
21. *Yad, loc. cit., Berashis Rabbah* 84:8, *Midrash Tehillim* 22:8, *Yalkut* 2:149, Rashi on Genesis 37:4, Ralbag on 2 Samuel 13:22.
22. *Sanhedrin* 3:5 (27b), *Yad, Rotzeach* 6:10, *Choshen Mishpat* 7:7 in *Hagah. Bertenoro on Makkos* 2:3. *Cf.* Rashash, *Sandhedrin loc. cit.* from Deuteronomy 19:4.
23. *Cheredim,* negative 1:19.
24. *Midrash Tehillim* 28:8. *Cf. Jeremiah* 9:7.
25. *Archin* 16b, *Tosefos ad loc.* "*Anavah*", *Yad, Deyos* 6:9, *Kitzur Shulchan Aruch* 29:18.
26. *Zohar* 3:85b, *Yad Deyos* 6:7. *Cf. Shabbos* 24a, *Gittin* 7a, *Orech Chaim* 260:4, *Magen Avraham* 260:2, *Mishnah Berurah* 260:10.
27. *Zohar, Yad, loc. cit.*
28. *Archin* 16b, *Tanchuma, Mishpatim* 7.
29. *Zohar* 3:86a, *Reshis Chochmah loc. cit.* 228a.
30. *Devarim Rabbah* 1:6, from Proverbs 24:25, *Tanna DeBei Eliahu Rabbah* 3 (30b), *Reshis Chochmah loc. cit.* 228b.
31. *Baba Metzia* 31a, *Archin* 16b, Rif, *Baba Metzia* 17a, *Yad, Deyos* 6:7.
32. *Chinuch* 239, *Minchas Chinuch ad loc.* 239:2, *Biur Halachah* 608:2 "*Ad.*"
33. *Archin* 16b, *Yad, Deyos* 6:7, *Kesef Mishneh, Lechem Mishnah, ad loc., Orech Chaim* 608:2 in *Hagah, Mishnah Berurah* 608:11, *Shaarey Tzion ad loc.* No. 13. Other, however, require that correction be continued until the other person actually strikes back physically, see *Hahahos Maimoni, Deyos* 6:7 No. 5, from *Elicha Rabbah* 2:4, *Tanchuma Tazria* 9; *Zohar* 1:68a, *Birkey Yosef, Machzik Berachah, Orech Chaim* 608, *Tshuvos Chaim Shoel* 2:43.
34. *Shnei Luchos HaBris loc. cit.* 1:2b, from Proverbs 9:8.
35. *Yad, Deyos* 6:7.
36. *Yebamos* 65b, *Yerushalmi, Terumah* 5:3 (30b), *Yerushalmi Sotah* 8:2 (34b). *Cf. Maaseh Choshev, Archin* 16b, quoted in *Makor Chesed* (on *Sefer Chasidim*) 413:4.
37. *Magen Avraham* 608:3, *Mishnah Berurah* 608:11.
38. *Zohar* 3:85b, *Reshis Chochmah loc. cit.* 228a.
39. *Ibid.,* Maharsha, *Archin* 16b "*Yachul.*"
40. *Yad, Deyos* 6:8, *Lechem Mishneh ad loc., Sefer Mitzvos Gadol,* negative 6, *Chinucht* 240, *Kitzur Shulchan Aruch* 29:17. *Cf. Berachos* 19b, *Kelayin* 10:24, *Yoreh Deah* 303:1.
41. *Yad, loc. cit.* Others, however, hold that a person should only be publicly

corrected one time. See *Zohar loc. cit.*, *Rav Shulchan Aruch* 608:5, *Baba Kama* 92b.

42. *Sefer Mitzvos Katan* 112, *Magen Avraham* 608:3, *Mishnah Berurah* 608:10.

43. *Cf. Minchas Chinuch* 240:1.

44. *Archin* 16b, *Tanchuma Mishpatim* 7, *Yad, Deyos* 6:8, *Sefer HaMitzvos,* negative 303, *Sefer Mitzvos Gadol (Smag)* negative 6, *Chinuch* 240, *Sefer Chasidim* 1125.

45. *Sefer Chasidim* 413, *Chinuch* 239, *Minchas Chinuch ad loc* 239:1, *Magen Avraham* 608:3, *Pri Chadash* 608:3, *Mishnah Berurah* 608:7, *Biur Halachah ibid.* "*Chayav*"; *Tshuvos Zecher Yehosef* 214, *Chavas Yair* 164, end, *Ksav Sofer, Even HaEzer* 47. *Cf. Tanna De Bei Eliahu Rabbah* 18 (91a), *Yalkut* 1:613, *Reshis Chochmah loc. cit.* 288a. Also see *Yoreh Deah* 334:48 in *Hagah,* quoting Mahariv 157, *Pishey Tshuvah ad loc.* quoting *Bechor Shor, Sotah* 47b; *Choshen Mishpat* 12:1 in *Hagah,* HaGra *ad loc.* 12:4, from *Kiddushin* 71a.

46. *Sefer Chasidim* 1125. *Cf. Akedah* 20.

47. *Turey Zahav, Orech Chaim* 603:2.

48. Ritva, *Yebamos* 65b, *Nimukey Yosef, Yebamol* (Rif 21b) "*Davar,*" *Orech Chaim* 608:2 in *Hagah,* from *Shabbos* 55a, *Eicha Rabbah* 2:4. *Cf. Shnei Luchos HaBris loc. cit,* note on 1:2b; *Mishneh Berurah* 608:9, *Birkey Yosef* 608:2, *Biur Halachah ibid.* "*Mochin.*"

49. *Yebamos* 65b, *Yerushalmi Terumah* 5:3 (30b), *Yerushalmi Chagigah* 1:8 (8a), *Yerushalmi Sotah* 8:2(34b).

50. *Baba Metzia* 31a, Rif 17a, *Lechem Mishneh, Mishneh LaMelech, Deyos* 6:7, *Minchas Chinuch* 239:4.

51. Even a rabbinical law, *Terumas HaDeshen* 43, *Yoreh Deah* 242:22 in *Hagah, Sifsey Cohen* 242:24, HaGra 242:58, Maharitz Chayos, *Berachos* 16b.

52. *Sefer Chasidim* 5.

53. *Berachos* 19b, *Eruvin* 68a, *Shavuos* 30b, *Sanhedrin* 82a, *Yad, Edos* 1:2.

54. Regarding a parent, see *Kiddushin* 32a, *Sanhedrin* 81a, *Yad, Mamrim* 6:11, *Chayay Adam* 68:10, *Kitzur Shulchan Aruch* 143:10. Regarding a teacher or rabbi, see *Yad, Talmud Torah* 5:9, *Yoreh Deah* 242:22. *Cf. Berachos* 2:5, 6, 7 (16a, b), *Tosefos, Chulin* 30b, "Lamdenu," HaGra *Yoreh Deah* 242:58, Maharitz Chayos, *Berachos* 16b, *Chulin* 30b.

55. *Eruvin* 67b, *Yoreh Deah* 242:22 in *Hagah. Cf. Pischey Tshuvah* 242:12, quoting *Yom Teruah* page 10 *Amar.*"

56. *Eruvin* 63a, *Yad, Talmud Torah* 5:3, *Yoreh Deah* 242:11.

57. *Sefer Yereyim* 223, *Sefer Mitzvos Katan* 112, *Sefer Mitzvos Gadol,* positive 11, *Hagahos Maimoni, Deyos* 6:7, *Magen Avraham* 608:3, *Mishnah Berurah* 608:5. Others, however, do not require correction in such a case, *cf. Sefer Mitzvos Gadol, Hagahos Maimoni, loc. cit., Tosefta Baba Basra* 2:6, *Pri Megadim, Eshel Avraham* 608:1, *Eliahu Rabbah, Orech Chaim* 608.

58. *Ibid.,* from *Shabbos* 65a.

59. Rashba, Meiri, *Betza* 30a, Ran, *Betva* (Rif 16b) "VeHach", Rosh, *Betza* 4:2, quoting *Sefer HaIttur, Orech Chaim* 608:2 in *Hagah, Rav Shulcan Aruch* 608:5, *Pri Megadim,* introduction 4:9, *Minchas Chinuch* 239:3.

60. Rashba *loc. cit. Mishnah Berurah* 608:6. *Cf. Horios* 4a, *Sanhedrin* 33b, Rambam on *Horios* 1:3 *Yad Sanhedrin* 110:9; *Shnei Luchos Ha Bris loc. cit.* 1:2b; *Kiddushin* 24b, HaGra, *Orech Chaim* 608:2. *Cf. Chochmas Shlomo, Orech Chaim* 608:2, from *Yebamos* 49b, *Tosefos, ad loc. "Ashivehu."*

61. Ran, *Nedarim* 8a *"Ha," Shavuos* (Rif 10a) *"Malkin," Yoreh Deah* 239:6, Sifsey Cohen 236:3, HaGra 608:2.

62. *Sefer Mitzvos Gadol* 11, *Sefer Chasidim* 39, *Orech Chaim* 608:2 in *Hagah, Biur Halachah ibid. "VeDavka."* See Ritva, *Makkos* 20b, that this only applies to a positive commandment, cf. *Mitzvas Tochacha* 9, *Makor Chesed* (on *Sefer Chasidim*) 39:3.

63. *Shabbos* 148b, *Betza* 30a, *Baba Basra* 60b *Yad Shivisas Assar* 1:7, *Orech Chaim* 339:3 in *Hagah* 356:6, 608:2, *Yoreh Deah* 239:3, *Sifsey Cohen, Yoreh Deah* 39:37, 293:7; *Sefer Chasidim* 262, *Shaarey Tshuvah* 3:196. *Cf. Tshuvos Sh'vus Yaakov* 3;1.

64. *Tshuvos Meil Tzadakah* 19, quoted in *Machetzis HaShekel* 608:2; *Hagahos Baruch Frankel* 608:2, *Biur Halachah* 608:2 *"Davka".*

65. *Shitah Mekubetzes, Betza* 30a, quoting Ritva; quoted in *Machetzis HaShekel* 608:3.

66. *Tosefos, Shabbos* 55a, *"Af," Baba Basra* 60b *"Mutav", Avodah Zarah* 4a *"SheHayah,"* Rosh, *Betza* 4:2, *Tshuvos HaRosh* 3:6, *Magen Avraham* 608:1.

67. *Levushey Serad* 608:2, *Mishneh Berurah* 608:3. *Cf. Orech Chaim* 365:6, *Magen Avraham* 365:12, *Machetzis HaShekel, Pri Megadim, ad loc., Mishneh Berurah* 365:30.

68. *Shitah Mekubetzes loc. cit.*, quoted in *Machetzis HaShekel* 608:3, *Yad Malachi* 2:434 (153b).

69. *Tashbatz* 2:47, quoted in *Shaarey Tzion* (on *Mishneh Berurah*) 608:3.

70. *Mordecai, Betza* 689. *Cf.* Rashi, *Betza* 30a *"Hanach."*

71. *Tashbatz, loc. cit.*, quoted in *Yad Malachi* 2:437 (153b), *Shaarey Tzion loc. cit.; Chochmas Shlomo, Orech Chaim* 608:2. *Cf. Sefer Chasidim* 262, *Magen Avraham* 263:30.

72. Regarding one who sins habitually out of desire, see *Biur Halachah* 608:2 *"Avel"* (end). See *Degel Marava. Yoreh Deah* 151.

73. *Kli Yakar ad loc., Tanna DeBei Eliahu Rabbah* 18 (91a), *Yalkut* 1:613, *Reshis Chochmah loc. cit.* 228a, *Minchas Chinuch* 239:4, *Biur Halachah, loc. cit. Cf. Baba Metzia* 58b, *Shavuos* 30a.

74. *Minchas Chinuch, loc. cit.*

75. *Cf. Tosefta Sanhedrin* 14:1, *Yad, Avodas Kochavrim* 4:6, *Migdal Oz, Kesef Mishneh, Pri Chadash, ad loc., Mordecai, Sanhedrin* 716, *Yoreh Deah* 340:5 in *Hagah,* 345:6 *Degel Marvava ad loc., Pischey Tshuvah* 340:5, 345:4, HaGra 340:13, 345:9, *Chochmas Adam* 156:7, *Kitzur Shulchan Aruch* 201:7; *Tshuvos Avodas HaGershoni* 48. Also see *Simchos* 3:5, *Yoreh Deah* 344:6.

76. As for example, the children of the Karaites, *cf. Yad, Mamrim* 3:3, *Hagahos Mordecai, Yebamos* 107, *Yoreh Deah* 159:3. Others, however, count later generations of Karaites as apostates, *cf.* Radbaz on *Yad. Mamrim* 3:3, *Sifse Cohen, Yoreh Deah* 159:6, 266:17, 267:59, *Berurah* 55:47; *Tshuvos R. Aaron*

ibn Chaim 113, 125, *Mabit* 2:38, Tshuvos R. Betzalel 3 (end). Other
sources, however, seem to indicate that the later generations of the Karaites
were worse than the earlier ones *cf. Tosefos, Avodah Zarah* 26b *"AniBtl A
Zarah* 2:7, from *Yerushalmi Avodah Zarah* 5:4 (34a). Also see Rambam on
Chulin 1:1.

77. *Shabbos* 68a, b, *Shavuos* 5a, *Yerushalmi Shabbos* 7:1 (40a), *Yad, Shegagos*
2:6, 7:2, *Yoreh Deah* 159:6 in *Hagah.*

78. *Yad, Mamrim* 3:3, *Sefer Mitzvos Gadol* 217 (end). *Cf. Baba Metzia* 33b.

79. *Cf. Kesubos* 41b, *Yerushalmi Sotah* 4:4 (20a), *BaMidbar Rabbah* 9:10, *Yad.
Issurey Biah* 1:9. See *Magen Avraham* 204:20, *Biur HaGra ibid. "Im Ansuhu."* Also see *Terumas HaDeshen* 223.

80. Regarding their portion in the World to Come, see *Sanhedrin* 110b, *Tosefta
Sanhedrin* 13:1, *Yalkut* 2:874, *Sotah* 48a end. From Rashi, *Sotah* 48b,
Sanhedrin 110b *"Ketaney",* this would appear to refer only to those who die
as children. *Cf. Koheles Rabbah* 4;1, *Zohar* 2:113a. Also see *Zohar* 2:96a,
3:234a.

81. Rambam, *Iggeres HaShmad,* p. 20, from Proverbs 6:30; *Yad Mamrim* :3:3,
Tshuvos Rashbash 68, quoted in *Pischey Tshuvah, Yoreh Deah* 268:10. *Cf.
Chazon Ish, Yoreh Deah* 13:28, *Even HaEzer, Yibum* 71, commentary on
Yad, Deyos 6:3.

82. *Sefer HaMitzvos,* positive 205, Maharitz Chayos, *Shabbos* 3a. *Cf Shaarey
Tzion* (on *Mishna Berurah*) 347:5.

83. *Yad, Kelayim* 10:29, *Yoreh Deah* 303:1, from *Berachos* 19b, 20a; *Yerushalmi
Kelayim* 9:1 (40a), *Yalkut* 1:911, 1:932; Rabenu Shimson (Rash) on *Kelayim*
9:4. *Cf. Baba Kama* 28a, *Yad. Avadim* 3:5. Also see *Tshuvos Shaagas Aryeh*
58.

84. Rosh, *Niddah* (laws of *Kelayim*) 9:6, *Yoreh Deah* 301:1 in *Hagah,* 372:1 in
Hagah, Sifsey Cohen 303:2; *Terumas HaDeshen* 285. Others, however,
dispute this, and require action even in such a case, see *Shaagas Aryeh* 58,
Pischey Tshuvah 303:1, *Yad Avraham ibid.*

85. *Berachos* 19b, Rashi *ad loc. "Kall,"* Minachos 38a, R. Yonah, *Berachos* (Rif
11b) *"Poshto", Yoreh Deah* 303:1, *Orech Chaim* 13:3.

86. But otherwise, one must take action even in such cases, *Nachalas Zvi, Yoreh
Deah* 303:1, *Pischey Tshuvah* 303:2.

87. *Brachos* 19b, *Shabbos* 81b, 94a, *Eruvin* 41b, *Megillah* 3b, *Minachos* 37b,
Yad, loc. cit.

88. *Tshuvos Nodeh Be Yehudah, Orech Chaim* 1:35, quoted in *Yad Avraham loc.
cit. Cf. Tshuvos Panim Meiros* 2:56, *Chavas Yair* 95.

89. *Sefer Chasidim* 405, *Yoreh Deah* 334:48 in *Hagah, Choshen Mishpat* 12:1 in
Hagan. See note 45.

90. *Shabbos* 54b, *Avodah Zarah* 18a, *Shavuos* 39b, *Yerushalmi Kesubos* 13:1
(68a), *Sh'mos Rabbah* 27:8, *Tanchuma, Mishpatim* 7, *Tazria* 9, *Midrash
Tehillim* 12:2, *Yalkut* 2:264, Rif. *Baba Metzia* 17a, *Yad Deyos* 6:7 *Yoreh Deah*
157:1 in *Hagah,* 334:48 in *Hagah, Sefer Chasidim* 5, *Shaarey Tshuvah* 3:195.
Cf. Avodah Zarah 4a, *Sanhedrin* 20a, *Yerushalmi Sotah* 1:8 (7b), *Eicha
Rabbah* 2:4, *Pesikta* 4 (33a), *Yalkut* 2:656. Also see *Eicha Rabbah* 1:34,

Yalkut 1:1012, *Mesilas Yesharim* 19 (28b). *Cf. Zohar* 3:46b, 3:218a, *Zohar Chadash* Ruth 77a.

91. Radak *ad loc., Sefer Yereyim* 223, *Sefer Mitzvos Gadol*, positive 11. *Cf.* Ezekiel 33:8.

92. Ramban *ad. loc., Yerushalmi Sotah* 7:4 (31a), *VaYikraRabbah* 25:1, *Magen Gibborim* 149.

93. *Rav Shulchan Aruch* 608:5.

94. *Sefer Chasidim* 5, 153. *Cf.* Ezekiel 33:9, Isaiah 49:4, 5; *Zohar* 1:58a.

95. *Yerushalmi Sotah* 7:4 (31a), *VaYikra Rabbah* 25:1, *Sefer Chasidim* 5.

96. *Tamid* 28a, *Tanchuma, Mishpatim* 7.

97. *BaMidbar Rabbah* 9:46, *Yoreh Deah* 246:1 in *Hagah, Shnei Luchos HaBris, Mesechta Shavuos* (2:96a), *Birkey Yosef, Yoreh Deah* 246:1, *Pischey Tshuvah* 246:3, *Rabenu Yerucham* 52, *Tshuvas Maharam Alshaker* 101, *Tshvuos Maaseh Chivah* 16. See *Baba Basra* 9a, *Sh'mos Rabbah* 35:3, *Yad, Matnos Aniyim* 10:6, *Yoreh Deah* 249:5.

98. *Berashis Rabbah* 99:1, *VaYikra Rabbah* 25:1, *Zohar* 3:150a, *Yoreh Deah* 246:1 in *Hagah*, *HaGra ad loc.* 246:7. *Cf. Berashis Rabbah* 75:5, *Pesachim* 53b, Rashi on Genesis 49:13; *Targum J.*, Rashi, on Deuteronomy 33:18, *Yalkut* 2:934; Rashi, *Sotah* 21a, *Zevachim* 2a, "Shimon," Bertenoro on *Zevachim* 1:2, *Taharos* 8:7 "*Shimon*", *Seder HaDoros* p. 121a.

99. *Sotah* 21a (end), from Song of Songs 8:7, *Yoreh Deah, Sh'nei Luchos HaBris, loc. cit.*

100. *Cf. Zohar Chadash* 33a, quoted in *Reshis Chochmah, Shaar Ha Yirah* 13 (37b).

101. *Tosefta, Makkos* 3:7, 8, 9; *Yad, Kelayim* 10:31 *Nazir* 5:20, *Avel* 3:5, Radbaz, *Kesef Mishneh, ad loc.*, HaGra, *Yoreh Deah* 303:3, *Minchas Chinuch* 263:14, 551:2, *Or HaChaim* on Leviticus 21:1. *Cf. Nazir* 44a, *Yad, Avodas Kochavim* 12:16. Regarding *Korais*, see *Sifra* on Leviticus 17:14.

102. *Cf.* Proverbs 26:27.

103. *Yoreh Deah* 157:1 in *Hagah*, 334:48 in *Hagah*, from *Tshuvos Mahariv* 156; HaGra 157:5, from *Sanhedrin* 73a. See *Pischey Tshuvah* 157:5.

103a. See *Chomas HaDas*, Introduction, note 1.

104. *Choshen Mishpat* 12:1 in *Hagah*, from *Kiddushin* 71a.

105. *Bechor Shor, Sotah* 47b, quoted in *Pischey Tshuvah* 334:19.

106. *Cf. Sanhedrin* 6b, *Yad, Sanhedrin* 22:1, *Sefer HaMitzvos*, negative 276, *Sefer Mitzvos Gadol*, negative 207, *Chinuch* 415, *Choshen Mishpat* 12:1, *Shaarey Tshuvah* 3:33.

107. *Shabbos* 4a, *Kiddushin* 55b, *Minachos* 48a, *Tosefta Challah* 1:8, *Magen Avraham* 454:21, 596:3, 655:0, *Chayay Adam* 148:18, *Mishneh Berurah* 655:3, *Shaarey Tzion ad loc.* 655:5.

108. *Magen Avraham* 254:21, *Mishneh Berurah* 254:40, *Tshuvos Tashbatz* 3:37, 38; *Tshuvos Besamim Rosh* 38, *Tshuvos Bais Yaakov* 88, Maharit. Chayos, *Shabbos* 4a.

109. *Tosefos. Shabbos* 4a, "*VeKi*", *Eruvin* 32b "*VeLo*", *Maharitz Chayos ad loc.*, *Cf. Yoreh Deah* 334:3 in *Hagah*, *HaGra ad loc.*, 334:5 from *Kiddushin* 172b, *Turey Zahav* 334:1, *Pischey Tshuvah* 334:1, *Tashbatz* 2:47; *Tshuvos Shemesh*

Tzadakah, Yoreh Deah 48, *Chavas Yair* 141, *Tshuvos Yaabatz* 1:79, *Tshuvos Radbaz* (new) 187, *Tshuvos Chasam Sofer* 322. Also see *Sefer Chasidim* 263, *Makor Chesed ad loc.* 263:1, *Magen Avraham* 638:4, *Beer Hetiv* 638:4, *Mishneh Berurah* 638:11, *Bikurey Yaakov* 638:9.

110. *Magen Avraham* 596:3, *Pri Megadim ad loc.*

111. Some say only a rabbinical law, *cf. Tshuvos Bais Yaakov* 88 end, *Mishneh LaMelech, Terumos* 3:17, *Maharitz Chayos, Eruvin* 32b.

112. *Eruvin* 32b.

113. *Tosefos. loc. cit., Gittin* 41b, *Chagigah* 2b "*Kofin,*" *Mahartiz Chayos ad loc., Hagahos Ashri, Shabbos* 1:3, *Magen Avraham* 306:29, *Machatzis HaShekel* 254:21.

114. *Magen Avraham* 252:21, *Rav Shulchan Aruch* 306:29.

115. *Eurvin* 69b, *Chulin* 5a, *Yerushalmi Nedarim* 3:9 (12b), *Tanchuma Ki Tisa* 33, *Zohar* 2:47a, *Yad Shabbo* 30:15, *Shaarey Tshuvah* 3:142, *Magen Avraham* 306:29, *Kitzur Shulchan Aruch* 72:1.

116. For a discussion whether this includes things that are not actually work, see *Machatzis HaShekel* 306:29, *Pri Megadim, Eshel Avraham* 306:29, *Shaarey Tzion* (on *Mishnah Berurah*) 306:50.

117. Regarding saving oneself, see *Pri Megadim, Mishbetzos Zahav* 328:5.

118. This even included idolatry, *cf. Magen Avraham* 306:29, *Mishnah Berurah* 306:48, 328:31. Others, however, apparently dispute this, see *Levush* 306, quoted in *Pri Megadim, Mishbetzos Zahav* 306:5.

119. *Orech Chaim* 328:10 in *Hagah, Magen Avraham* 306:29, *Turey Zahav* 306:5, 328:4, *HaGra, Orech Chaim* 306:14.

120. But not for a positive commandment, see *Rav Shulchan Aruch* 306:29. *Cf. Rosh HaShanah* 4:8 (32b), *Yad, Shofar* 1:4 *Orech Chaim* 586:21, *Magen Avraham* 586:23, *Turey Zahav* 655:2, *Mishneh Berurah* 586:83.

121. *Rav Shulchan Aruch* 306:29.

122. *Tosefos loc. cit., Pesachim* 88b "*Kofin,*" from *Berachos* 47b, *Magen Avraham* 306:29, quoting *Tshovos Bais Yosef* 2, *Chayay Adam* B 68:14. Also see *Magen Avraham* 426:2, *Maharitz Chayos, Rosh HaShanah* 38b. *Cf. Rosh Berachos* 7:20, *Magen Avraham* 90:30, *Tshuvos Besamin Rosh* 155, *Tshuvos Shaagas Aryeh* 96, 97, *Maharitz Chayos, Berachos* 47b.

123. Even where actual work is involved, *Rav Shulchan Aruch* 306:29, *Chayay Adam* B 68:12, *Mishnah Berurah* 306:57.

124. *Orech Chaim* 306:14, 329:8 in *Hagah*, from *Tosefos loc. cit: Magen Avraham* 306:28, *Turey Zahav* 306:5, *Kitzur Shulchan Aruch* 92:10.

125. *Shabbos* 151b, *Yoma* 85b, *Yerushalmi Yoma* 8:5 (41b) *Magen Avraham* 396:29, *Mishneh Berurah* 306:57.

126. *Pri Megadim, Mishbetzos Zahav* 306:5, *Rav Shulchan Aruch* 306:29, *Kuntres Acharon ad loc.* No. 1.

127. *Shabbos* 121a, *Yebamos* 114a, *Gottin* 55a, *Niddah* 46b; *Yad, Shabbos* 12:7, *Maachalos Assuros* 17:27, *Avel* 3:12, *Orech Chaim* 343:1, *Yoreh Deah* 373:1 in *Hagah*. Also see *Yad, Shabbos* 24:11, *Rav Shulchan Aruch* 343:1, *Chayay Adam* 66:3.

128. Even where the minor wishes to voluntarily leave the Jewish fold, he is not considered doing so purposefully, *Shaarey Tzion* (on *Mishneh Berurah*) 306:49. Cf. *Machetzis HaShekel* 596:3. See *Yebamos* 33b, 61b, *Yerushalmi Pesachism* 8:1 (57b), *Yerushalmi Sotah* 1:2 (3a), 2:1 (9a), Raavard, *Sotah* 2:4, *Issurey Biah* 3:2, *Tosefos, Kesubos* 9a *"Vely,"* 40b *"Hah."*

129. *Magen Avraham* 306:29, *Mishneh Berurah* 306:57. Others, however, only allow the violation of a Biblical law in the case of a minor when it is certain that he will be saved, *Chayay Adam* 66:3, *Nishmas Adam ad loc.* No. 1 Cf. *Eliahu Rabbah* 306, from *Eruvin* 103b.

130. *Orech Chaim* 306:14.

131. Some authorities, however, have exactly the reverse of this opinion, and maintain that one may only violate the Sabbath for a person who wishes to leave the fold willingly, cf. Bach, *Orech Chaim* 306, *Magen Avraham* 306:29, *Machetzis HaShekel ad loc.* See *Kesubos* 3b.

132. *Eliahu Rabbah, Orech Chaim* 306:33, *Beer Hetiv* 305:5, quoting *Tshuvos Nachalas Shiva* 83; *Shaarey Tshuvah* 306:19, *Mishneh Berurah* 306:56, *Shaarey Tzion ad loc.* 306:47, from *Rosefos loc. cit.* Others, however, dispute this, cf. *Tshuvos Sh'vus Yaakov* 1:16, quoted in *Shaarey Tshuvah loc. cit.*

133. *Sefer Chasidim* 188. Cf. Radak *ad loc.*